CW01651043

ACCA

Strategic Business Leader (SBL)

Pocket Notes

KAPLAN PUBLISHING

British library cataloguing-in-publication data

A catalogue record for this book is available from the British Library.

Published by:
Kaplan Publishing UK
Unit 2 The Business Centre
Molly Millars Lane
Wokingham
Berkshire
RG41 2QZ

ISBN 978-1-83735-036-0

© Kaplan Financial Limited, 2025

Printed and bound in Great Britain.

The text in this material and any others made available by any Kaplan Group company does not amount to advice on a particular matter and should not be taken as such. No reliance should be placed on the content as the basis for any investment or other decision or in connection with any advice given to third parties. Please consult your appropriate professional adviser as necessary. Kaplan Publishing Limited and all other Kaplan group companies expressly disclaim all liability to any person in respect of any losses or other claims, whether direct, indirect, incidental, consequential or otherwise arising in relation to the use of such materials.

All rights reserved. No part of this publication may be reproduced, stored in a retrieval system, or transmitted, in any form or by any means, electronic, mechanical, photocopying, recording or otherwise, without the prior written permission of Kaplan Publishing.

Contents

Syllabus

Aim

To demonstrate organisational leadership and senior consultancy or advisory capabilities and relevant professional skills, through the context of an integrated case study.

Main Capabilities

On successful completion of this paper, candidates should be able to:

A Apply excellent leadership and ethical skills to set the 'tone from the top' and promote a positive culture within the organisation, adopting a whole organisation perspective in managing performance and value creation.

B Evaluate the effectiveness of the governance and agency system of an organisation and recognise the responsibility of the board or other agents towards their stakeholders, including the organisation's social responsibilities and the reporting implications.

C Evaluate the strategic position of the organisation against the external environment and the availability of internal resources, to identify feasible strategic options.

D Analyse the risk profile of the organisation and of any strategic options identified, within a culture of responsible risk management.

E Select and apply appropriate information technologies and data analytics, to analyse factors affecting the organisation's value chain to identify strategic opportunities and implement strategic options within a framework of robust IT security controls.

F Evaluate management reporting and internal control and audit systems to ensure compliance and the achievement of organisation's objectives and the safeguarding of organisational assets.

G Apply high level financial techniques from Applied Skills exams in the planning, implementation and evaluation of strategic options and actions.

H Enable success through innovative thinking, applying best in class strategies and disruptive technologies in the management of change; initiating, leading and organising projects, while effectively managing talent and other business resources.

I Apply a range of Professional Skills in addressing requirements within the Strategic Business Leader examination and in preparation for, or to support, current work experience.

J Demonstrate other employability and digital skills in preparing for and taking SBL examinations

The Examination

The SBL exam is based on an integrated case study. Pre-seen information is provided two weeks in advance of the exam date.

The primary aim of the pre-seen is to enable students to become familiar with the business activities of the case study organisation and the industry in which it operates. Familiarity with this important contextual information will help students to better understand and apply the further information that will be provided via exhibits in the SBL exam.

The SBL exam will contain further new information in the form of exhibits, which students should focus on in answering the requirements. The exhibits in the exam may take a variety of forms including memos, emails, briefing notes, interview extracts, we pages, financial reports etc.

The SBL exam has three compulsory tasks, with each task having a varying numbers of parts and total marks.

These assignments or tasks may require the candidate to take on different roles, depending on the situation. The number of marks allocated to all these assignments or the
sub-parts of these will add up to 100 in total.

Within the total marks available, there are professional skills marks. All five professional skills will be tested at each examination sitting and will be worth 20 marks in total.

Each professional skill will be tested only once and will be worth four marks. All tasks must be completed.

The SBL exam time is 3 hours and 15 minutes which includes Reading, Planning and Reflection time (RPRT). This time can be used flexibly at any time during the exam.

Number of marks 100

Three compulsory tasks with a varying number of parts.

Total time allowed: 3 hours 15 minutes.

NB More detail on exam guidance in Chapter 1

Quality and accuracy are of the utmost importance to us so if you spot an error in any of our products, please send an email to mykaplanreporting@kaplan.com with full details, or follow the link to the feedback for in MyKaplan.

Our Quality Co-ordinator will work with our technical team to verify the error and take action to ensure it is corrected in future editions.

chapter

1

Introduction to the SBL exam

In this chapter

- Overview.
- Being a leader.
- Thinking strategically.
- Communication.
- Commercial acumen.
- Analysis.
- Scepticism.
- Evaluation.

Overview

Being a leader
Thinking strategically
The Strategic Leader
INTRODUCTION TO THE SBL EXAM
Professional skills
Communication
Commercial acumen
Analysis
Scepticism
Evaluation

Being a leader

As a leader, you are expected to be able to analyse a business situation and provide and implement appropriate, effective and sustainable solutions.

This means that you can

- be clear and focussed, identifying the key issues in any situation
- analyse and address ethical concerns
- use technical models and quantitative analysis to draw out key issues, establish causality and integrate a wide range of factors into a coherent argument
- make recommendations that meet the needs of users and are 'fit for purpose'.

Thinking strategically

Having a strategic perspective means that you can do the following:

- Take a **long term** perspective.
- Look at the **whole organisation** as well as individual products /divisions / SBUs.
- Set the direction of the whole organisation and **integrate** its activities.
- Consider the views of **all stakeholders**, not just shareholders.
- Analyse the organisation's **resources** and define resource requirements.
- Relate the organisation to its **environments**.
- Look at gaining a sustainable **competitive advantage.**

Communication

Syllabus spec

(a) **Inform** concisely, objectively, and unambiguously, while being sensitive to cultural differences, using appropriate media and technology.

(b) **Persuade** using compelling and logical arguments demonstrating the ability to counter argue when appropriate.

(c) **Clarify** and simplify complex issues to convey relevant information in a way that adopts an appropriate tone and is easily understood by the intended audience.

In summary, this means you have to express yourself clearly and convincingly through the appropriate medium while being sensitive to the needs of the intended audience.

Commercial acumen

Syllabus spec

(a) **Demonstrate awareness** of organisational and wider external factors affecting the work of an individual or a team in contributing to the wider organisational objectives.

(b) **Use judgement** to identify key issues in determining how to address or resolve problems and in proposing and recommending the solutions to be implemented.

(c) **Show insight and perception** in understanding work-related and organisational issues, including the management of conflict, demonstrating acumen in arriving at appropriate solutions or outcomes.

In summary, this means you have to show awareness of the wider business and external factors affecting business, using commercially sound judgement and insight to resolve issues and exploit opportunities.

Analysis

Syllabus spec

(a) **Investigate** relevant information from a wide range of sources, using a variety of analytical techniques to establish the reasons and causes of problems, or to identify opportunities or solutions.

(b) **Enquire** of individuals or analyse appropriate data sources to obtain suitable evidence to corroborate or dispute existing beliefs or opinion and come to appropriate conclusions.

(c) **Consider** information, evidence and findings carefully, reflecting on their implications and how they can be used in the interests of the department and wider organisational goals.

In summary, this means you have to thoroughly investigate and research information from a variety of sources and logically process it with a view to considering it for recommending appropriate action.

Scepticism

Syllabus spec

(a) **Probe** deeply into the underlying reasons for issues and problems, beyond what is immediately apparent from the usual sources and opinions available.

(b) **Question** facts, opinions and assertions, by seeking justifications and obtaining sufficient evidence for their support and acceptance.

(c) **Challenge** information presented or decisions made, where this is clearly justified, in a professional and courteous manner; in the wider professional, ethical, organisational, or public interest.

In summary, this means you have to probe, question and challenge information and views presented to them, to fully understand business issues and to establish facts objectively, based on ethical and professional values.

Evaluation

Syllabus spec

(a) **Assess and use professional judgement** when considering organisational issues, problems or when making decisions; taking into account the implications of such decisions on the organisation and those affected.

(b) **Estimate** trends or make reasoned forecasts of the implications of external and internal factors on the organisation, or of the outcomes of decisions available to the organisation.

(c) **Appraise** facts, opinions and findings objectively, with a view to balancing the costs, risks, benefits and opportunities, before making or recommending solutions or decisions.

In summary, this means you have to carefully assess situations, proposals and arguments in a balanced way, using professional and ethical judgement to predict future outcomes and consequences as a basis for sound decision-making.

chapter

2

Concepts of strategy

In this chapter

- Strategic planning.
- The strategic planning process.
- Strategic drift.

Strategic planning

Benefits of strategic planning	Disadvantages of strategic planning
• Improves fit with the environment • Makes best use of scarce resources • Provides direction • Ensures goals are met • Can create competitive advantage • Ensures plans are properly implemented	• Time consuming • Becomes a straightjacket • Creates bureaucracy • Less relevant in a crisis

The strategic planning process

The 3 stage planning model (JSW)

Strategic analysis

- External analysis to identify opportunities and threats
- Internal analysis to identify strengths and weaknesses
- Stakeholder analysis to identify key objectives and to assess the power and interest of different groups
- Gap analysis to identify the difference between desired and expected performance.

Strategic choice

- Strategies are required to 'close the gap'
- Competitive strategy – for each business unit
- Directions for growth – which markets/ products should be invested in
- Whether expansion should be achieved by organic growth, acquisition or some form of joint arrangement.

Strategy into action (implementation)

- Structuring
- Enabling
- Change

Strategic drift

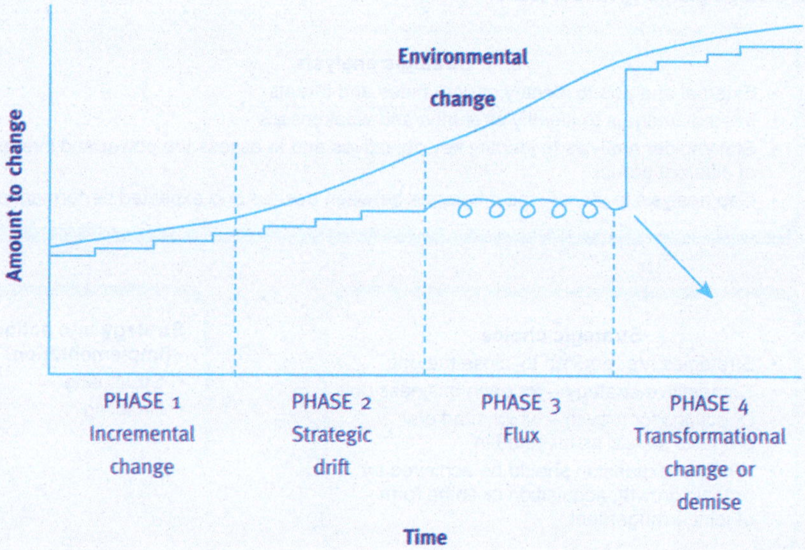

To avoid strategic drift:

- assess the environment for changes
- have flexible systems
- break down barriers to change
- have clear understanding of the mission and objectives
- have strong leaders

chapter

3

Strategic analysis

In this chapter

- PESTEL analysis.
- 5 Forces analysis.
- Porter's diamond.
- Critical success factors (CSFs).
- SWOT analysis.
- Value chain analysis.

PESTEL analysis

Key strategic use: to analyse potential impacts on future growth

Area of the model	Key factors to consider
Political	Changes to government policy
Economic	Booms or recessions
Social	Changes to taste/fashion
Technological	New hardware/software capabilities
Environmental	Geographic location or use of resources
Legal	Restrictions or extra regulations

5 Forces analysis

Key strategic use: to analyse potential impacts on future margins

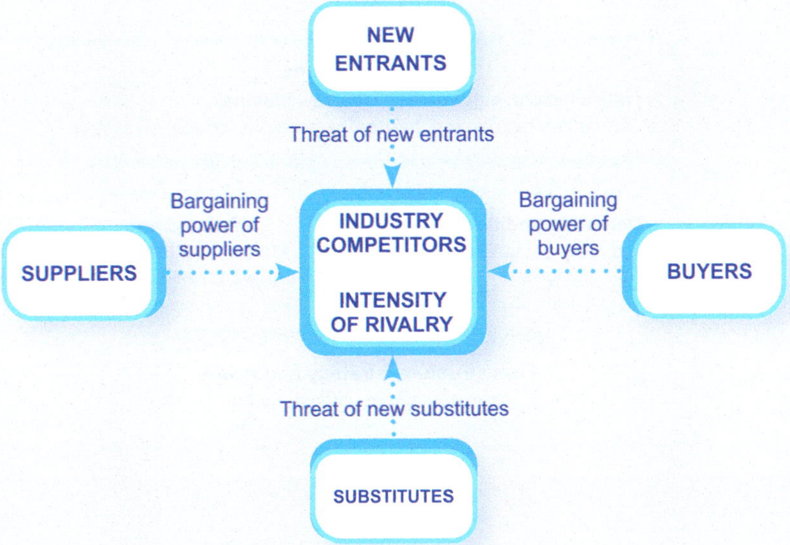

Porter's diamond

Key strategic use: to analyse potential new foreign markets for expansion

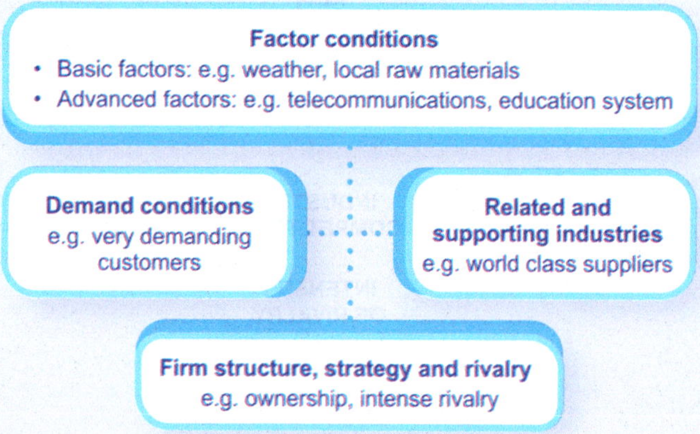

Critical success factors (CSFs)

CSFs are the essential areas of the business that must be performed well if the mission, objectives and goals of the business are to be achieved.

- What is critical to the company's success?
- What really matters to customers?
- What will lead to a sustainable competitive advantage (cost leader vs differentiator)?

Targets (KPIs) are then usually set to see if the company is succeeding in these vital areas.

SWOT analysis

Key strategic use: to bring together the internal and external analysis in order to understand overall strategic position

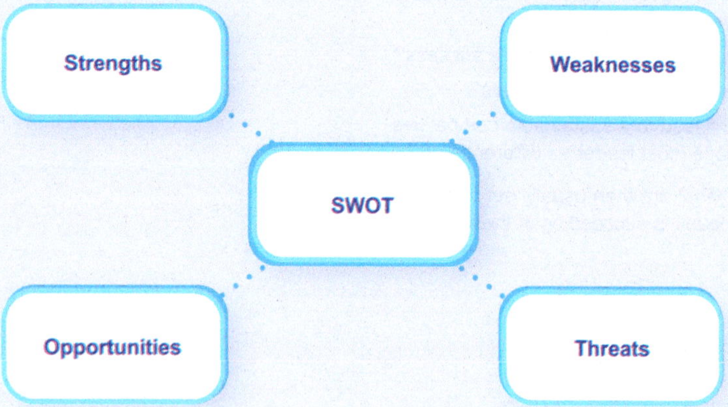

Value chain analysis

Key strategic use: to determine the source of competitive (dis)advantage

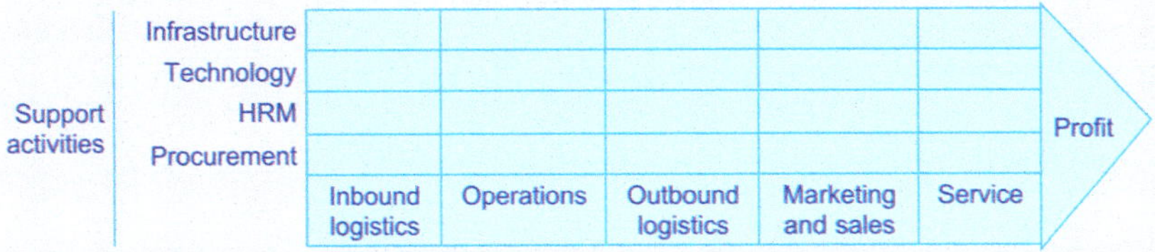

- Used to identify where competitive advantages can be gained.
- Look for 'weak links' in the chain to improve.

chapter

4

Performance analysis

In this chapter

- Mission, values and objectives.
- Quantitative analysis.
- Baldrige performance excellence.
- Benchmarking.

Missions, values and objectives

Mission statements

- States purpose and why they exist
- Helps set the tone and culture
- Communicates to stakeholders

Values

- States the core ethics and principles of the organisation
- Follows on from the mission statement
- Amazon's values include: Customer obsession, Think big and Hire and develop the best'

Objectives

- Specific targets to help ensure an organisation meets its mission in-line with its values
- Ideally targets should be 'SMART'
- These often align with CSFs and create measurable KPIs

Quantitative analysis

The quantitative information will typically include:

Financial Data

Specific marks will be available for interpreting financial ratios that can be calculated from the financial data.

The questions will never ask for specific ratios, but there will always be enough information to calculate and interpret several financial ratios.

The key will be to choose 3/4 key ratios and explain the cause of any changes and the effect that these changes might have on the organisation.

Non-financial data

Non-financial information will also be provided in tables, and candidates will be expected to use and interpret this information. Such tables will supplement, and to some extent replace, information traditionally given in the narrative scenario.

Key performance indicators (KPIs)

In order to measure performance against the CSFs an organisation will usually set a number of KPIs.

KPIs are quantifiable measures that are used to track and assess the performance of an organisation or department.

They will often be used as part of a '**balanced scorecard**' approach.

Balanced scorecard

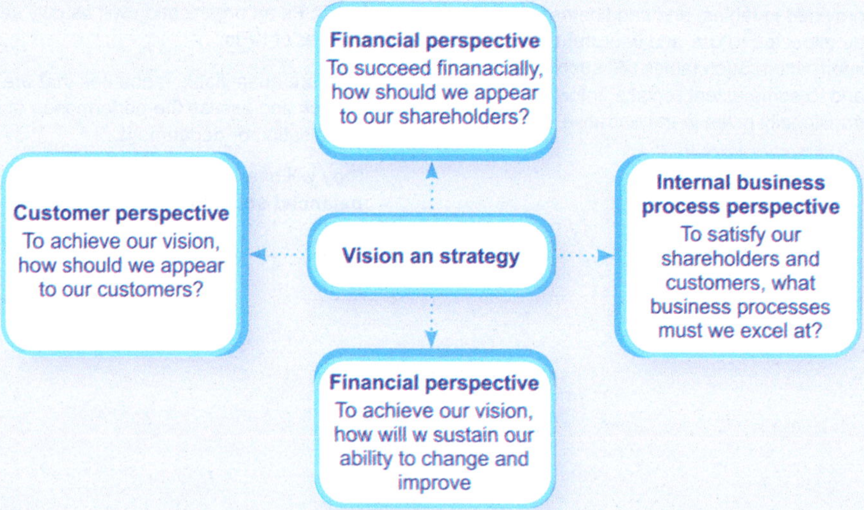

Baldrige performance excellence

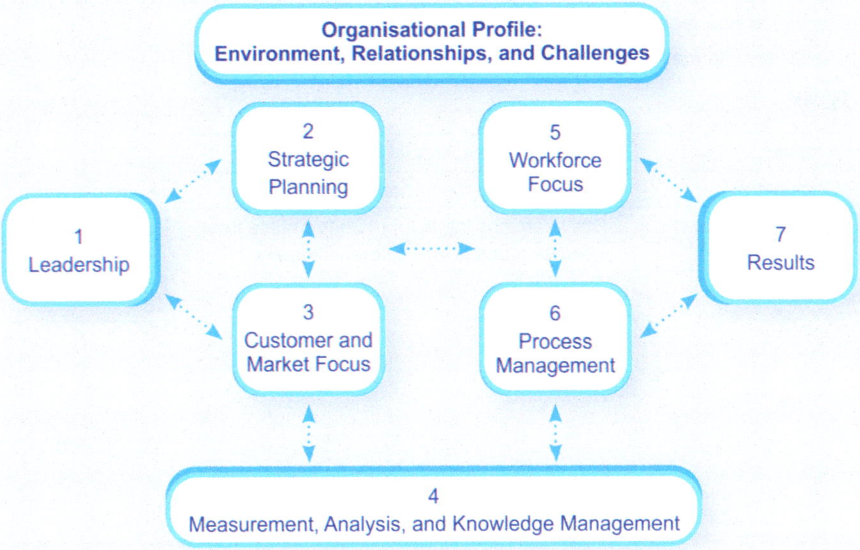

Benchmarking

- determines where improvements are required
- analyses how high performance is achieved
- uses this information to improve performace levels in processes

Types:

Internal	This determines internal best practice
Competitive	This examines the performance of rivals
Activity / best-in-class	This examines the level of performance from a similar process in a different industry

chapter

5

Strategic choice

In this chapter

- Competitive strategies.
- Growth strategies.
- Strategy evaluation.

Competitive strategies

A range of possible competitive positions is provided in the strategy clock:

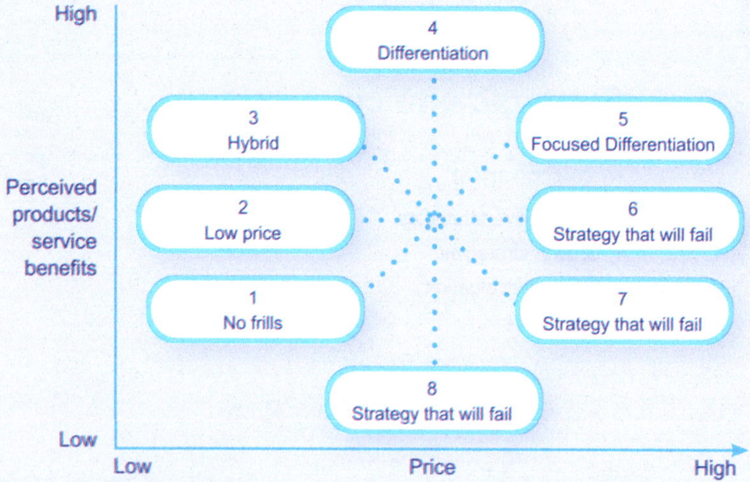

Competitive advantages are often simplified into three main categories – **Cost leader, Differentiation and Niche.**

Key elements of successful competitive strategies:

	CSFs	Key threats
Cost Leader	Finding cheaper alternatives Eliminating all waste Economies of scale A focus on cost reduction Branding Service levels	Changes in buyer preferences Loss of barriers to entry Larger (international?) rivals Loss of brand Difficult to achieve Target for all rivals
Differentiation	Innovation Branding Marketing	Being copied New technology which differentiates
Niche	Market knowledge Unique product/service	Recession Small market size Few barriers

Failing strategies fail because they are beaten by competitive rivals.

Growth strategies

These can be derived from the Ansoff matrix:

	Existing product	New product
Existing market	**Market penetration** – Introduce a new or improved competitive strategy – Best used when market is growing **Risks** – Competitors will react – Can lead to stagnation	**Product development** – Create new or improved products – Or copy rivals **Risks** – Unknown demand – Can harm existing products
New market	**Market development** – Target a new market segment – Strategic alliances are often used to reduce risks **Risks** – Puts a strain on capabilities – Need new external analysis	**Diversification** – New products and markets – Can be forward, backward, horizontal or conglomerate **Risks** – Very different CSFs – Need new external analysis – Can reduce flexibility

Strategy evaluation

- **Suitability** – is the strategy consistent, both externally and internally?
  - Does it give the firm a better fit with the environment?
  - Portfolio analysis – how do new products fit with existing ones?
  - Are their synergies with other parts of the business?
  - Is the timing right?
- **Acceptability** – is the strategy acceptable to the stakeholders?
  - Is the risk acceptable?
  - Is it ethical?
  - How will other stakeholders react?
- **Feasibility** – is the strategy within the resources and capability of the organisation?
  - Is the time-scale achievable?
  - Do we have the critical success factors necessary to implement the strategy?

chapter

6

Methods of strategic development

In this chapter

- Main methods of development.
- Portfolio analysis.

Main methods of development

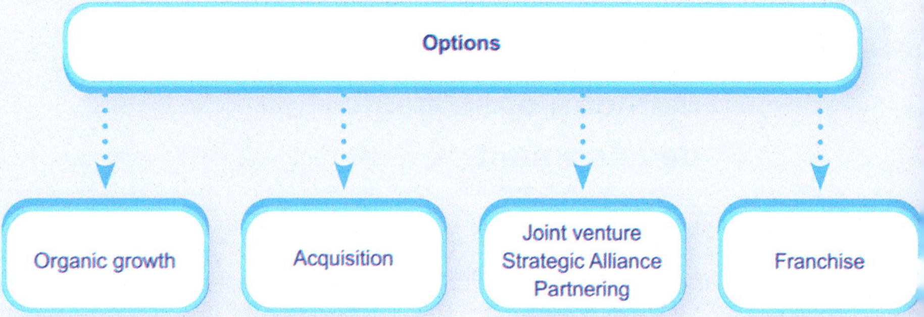

Organic growth	Acquisition	Joint venture / Strategic Alliance / Partnering	Franchise
Start from a zero base alone	Buy an existing business	Do it with a partner	Allow others to use the brand
Slow, but risky	Quick but expensive	Share skills and costs, but difficult to agree	Low cost, but lose control

Portfolio analysis

BCG matrix

Market growth

Market share	Low	High
High	**Cash-cow** • Strong position in a low growth (therefore unattractive) market • Little threat from rivals • Just keep the product ticking over and collect the cash	**Star** • Attractive market so have to reinvest heavily to defend market share and grow • Little cash surplus
Low	**Dog** • Too small to benefit from economies of scale • Market does not justify further investment • Divest	**Problem-child** • Attractive market but too small to capitalise on it. • Either invest heavily to gain market share or get out • 'Double or quit'

Ashridge parenting matrix

This model looks at the strategic fit between a parent company and the strategic business units it manages.

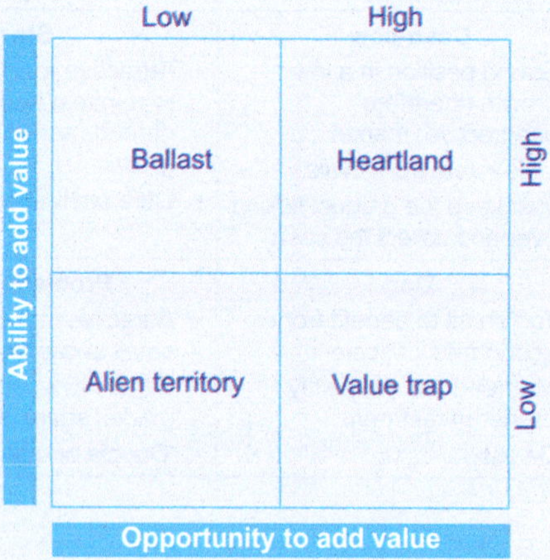

chapter

7

Governance

In this chapter

- Overview of corporate governance.
- Company ownership and control.
- Coverage of governance.
- Rules and principles based approaches to corporate governance.
- Key concepts.
- Purpose and scope of governance.
- Stakeholder theory.
- Stakeholder claim.
- Family structures.
- Insider-dominated structures.

Overview of Corporate Governance

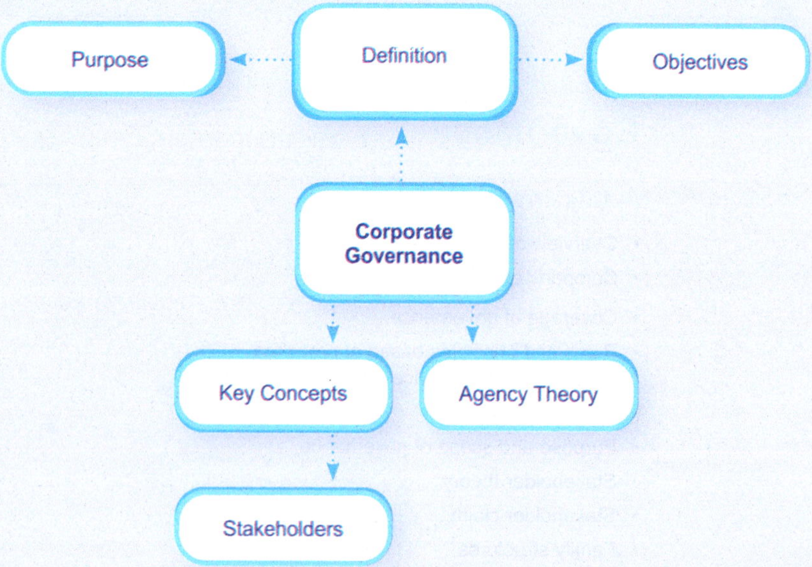

Company ownership and control?

- Corporate governance is the system by which companies are directed and controlled in the interests of shareholders and other stakeholders. This split of ownership and management can lead to agency costs.

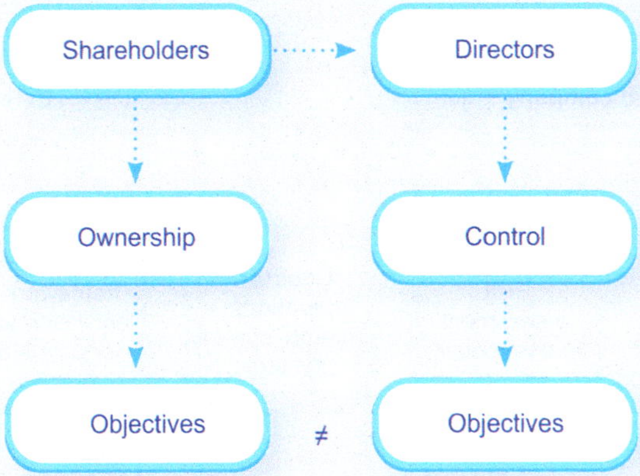

Coverage of governance

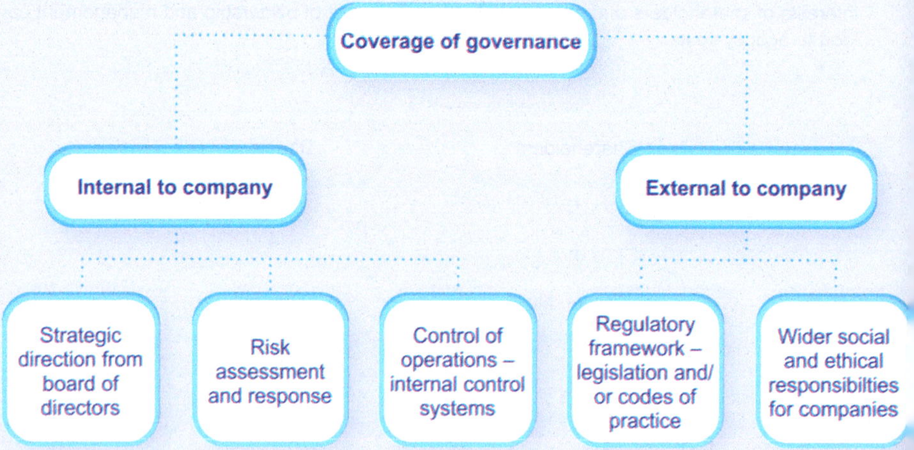

Rules and principles based approaches to corporate governance

- A rules-based approach instils the code into law with appropriate penalties for transgression.
- A principles-based approach requires the company to adhere to the spirit rather than the letter of the code. The company must either comply with the code or explain why it has not through reports to the appropriate body and its shareholders.

Choice of governance regime

The decision as to which approach to use for a country can be governed by many factors:

- dominant ownership structure (bank, family or multiple shareholder)
- legal system and its power/ability
- government structure and policies
- state of the economy
- culture and history
- levels of capital inflow or investment coming into the country
- global economic and political climate.

Comply or explain

A principles-based code requires the company to state that it has complied with the requirements of the code or to explain why it could not do so in its annual report. This will leave shareholders to draw their own conclusions regarding the governance of the company.

Key concepts

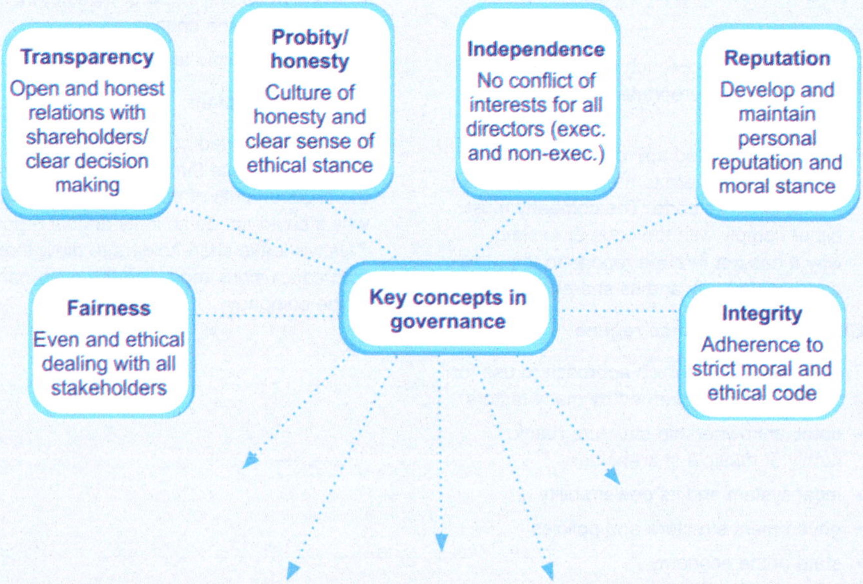

Innovation

- Innovation and experimentation in reporting
- The business moves away from rigid compliance towards the better communication of its individual value creation story for its providers of financial capital

Accountability

Provision of complete information to all stakeholders and effective risk management

Responsibility

- Acceptance of responsibility for governance decisions
- Clarity or roles and responsibilities

Judgement

Ability to make correct decision from many conflicting inputs

Scepticism

- Scepticism(often referred to as professional scepticism) is an attitude which includes a questioning mind
- To provide a critical assessment of evidence
- For example, non-executive directors apply scepticism in order to challenge and scrutinise management effectively

Purpose and scope of governance

For the private sector:

- to monitor those parties within a company which control the resources owned by investors.
- the primary objective of sound corporate governance is improved corporate performance and accountability in creating long term shareholder value.

For the public and not for profit sectors:

- objectives within these organisations are more complex and conflicting.
- organisations are often appraised according to the "value for money" (VFM) that they generate.
  - defined as performance of an activity to simultaneously achieve economy, efficiency and effectiveness.

The three elements of value for money are:

- **Economy** = a measure of inputs to achieve a certain service or level of service.
- **Effectiveness** = a measure of outputs, i.e. services/facilities.
- **Efficiency** = measure of outputs over inputs.

Stakeholder theory

- The basis for stakeholder theory is that companies are so large and their impact on society so pervasive that they should discharge accountability to many more sectors of society than solely their shareholders.
- Stakeholders are not only are affected by the organisation but they also affect the organisation.

Stakeholder claim

A stakeholder claim is where a stakeholder wants something from an organisation. These claims can be concerned with the way a stakeholder may want to influence the activities of an organisation or by the way they are affected by the organisation.

There are:

- Direct claims – made by stakeholders directly with the organisation and are unambiguous e.g. trade unions, they have their own voice.
- Indirect claims – where the stakeholder is "voiceless", e.g. an individual customer of a large retail organisation or the environment with the inevitable problem of interpretation.

Family structures

A family structure exists where a family has a controlling number of shares in a company.

Benefits

- Fewer agency costs – since the family is directly involved.
- Ethics – threats to reputation are threats to family honour, increases the likely level of ethical behaviour.
- Fewer short-term decisions – wealth already inherent in such families suggest long-term growth is a bigger issue.

Problems

- Gene pool – the gene pool of expertise in owner managers may be questionable over generations.
- Feuds – families fight, and this is an added element of cultural complexity.
- Separation – families separate and this could be costly in terms of buying out shareholding and restructuring.

Insider-dominated structures

Insider-dominated structures are where the listed companies are dominated by a small group of shareholders.

Benefits:

- The agency problem is reduced – i.e. establish links with owners and managers.
- Greater access to and potentially lower cost of capital i.e. smaller base of shareholders.
- Smaller base of shareholders willing to take a long term strategic view of investment.
- Improved communication and influence over management.

Problems:

- Lack of minority shareholder protection (unlike protection in law in outsider-dominated structures).
- Opaque operations and lack of transparency in reporting.
- Misuse of power i.e. reluctance to employ outsiders in influential positions and NED's.
- The market does not decide or govern (shareholders cannot exit easily to express discontent).
- Tend to be reluctant until forced to develop formal governance structures.
- Reluctance of large independent shareholders to invest.

chapter

8

The board of directors

In this chapter

- Board of directors.
- Non-executive directors.
- NEDs on the board.
- Chairperson and CEO.
- Board committees.
- Remuneration committee.
- Components of directors' remuneration package.
- Non-executive directors' remuneration.
- Audit committee roles.
- The role of the risk committee.

Board of directors

Roles and Responsibilities

- provide entrepreneurial leadership of the company
- represent company view and account to the public
- decide on a formal schedule of matters to be reserved for board decision
- determine the company's mission and purpose (strategic aims)
- select and appoint the CEO, chairman and other board members
- set the company's values and standards
- ensure that the company's management is performing its job correctly
- establish appropriate internal controls that enable risk to be assessed and managed
- ensure that the necessary financial and human resources are in place for the company to meet its objectives
- ensure that its obligations to its shareholders and other stakeholders are understood and met
- meet regularly to discharge its duties effectively.

For listed companies:

- appoint appropriate NEDs
- establish remuneration committee
- establish nominations committee
- establish audit committee
- assess its own performance and report it annually to shareholders
- submit themselves for re-election at regular intervals.

Provide leadership
Set the culture and 'tone' of the organisation
Determine mission, values and purpose
Internal controls
Roles and responsibilities
Strategic decisions
Compliance with laws and regulations
Board structure and appointments
Stakeholder and public relations

Non-executive directors

Roles and Responsibilities

- Strategy role – challenging strategy, offering advice and contributing toward strategic success.
- Scrutinising role – hold executive directors to account for decisions taken and results obtained.
- Risk role – ensure adequate system of internal controls and system of risk management in place.
- People role – oversee the appointment and remuneration of executive directors.

NEDs on the board

Advantages	Disadvantages
• monitoring role	• unity of the board
• additional expertise	• quality of NEDs
• enhanced perception of company	• liability of the role
• communication with stakeholders	
• discipline over strategy	

Structure of the Board

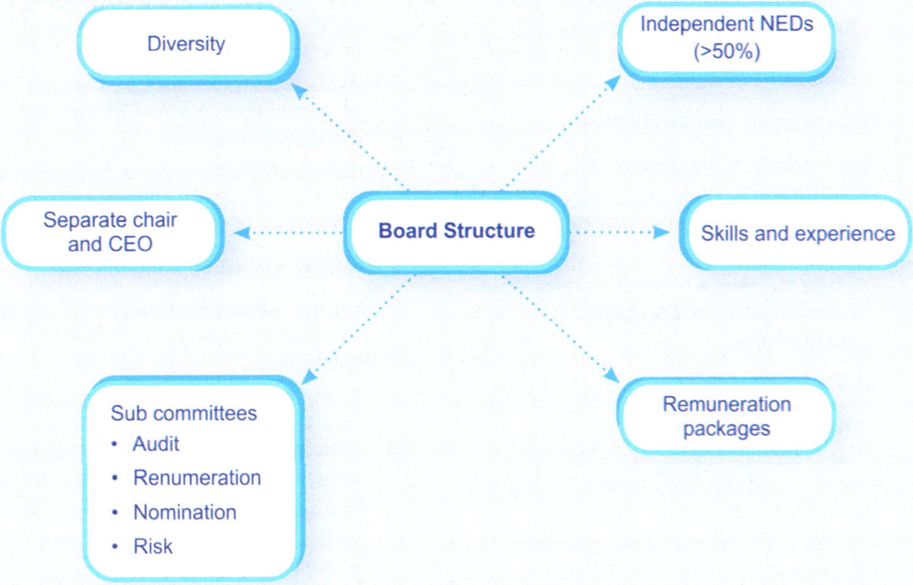

Chairperson and CEO

- 'A clear division of responsibilities must exist at the head of the company. No individual should have unfettered power of decision.'

Chairperson's responsibilities

Responsibility of the chairperson:

- ensure that the board sets and implements the company's direction and strategy effectively
- act as the company's lead representative, explaining aims and policies to the shareholders.

CEO's responsibilities

Responsibility of the CEO:

- take responsibility for the performance of the company, as determined by the board's strategy
- report to the chairperson and/or board of directors.

Reasons for splitting the role

- Representation: the chairperson is clearly and solely a representative of shareholders with no conflict of interest.
- Accountability: provides a clear path of accountability for the CEO and the management team.
- Temptation: reduces the temptation to act more in self-interest rather than purely in the interest of shareholders.

Reasons against splitting the role

Unity: the separation of the role creates two leaders rather than the unity provided by a single leader.

- Ability: both roles require an intricate knowledge of the company. It is far easier to have a single leader with this ability rather than search for two such individuals
- Human nature: there will almost inevitably be conflict between two high- powered executive offices.

Board committees

Importance of committees

Board sub-committees are a generally accepted part of board operations.

Positives:

- reduces board workload and enables them to improve focus on other issues.
- creates structures that can use inherent expertise to improve decisions in key areas.
- communicates to shareholders that directors take these issues seriously.
- increase in shareholder confidence.
- communicates to stakeholders the importance of remuneration and risk.
- satisfy requirements of the UK Corporate Governance Code (2018) (or other governance requirements).

Nominations committee

Responsibilities of nominations committee:

- regularly review the structure, size, skills, experience and composition of the board.
- consider the balance between executives and NEDs.
- ensure appropiate diversity at board level.
- provide an appropriate balance of power to reduce domination in executive selection by the CEO/Chairperson.
- full consideration to succession planning for directors.
- prepare a description of the role and capabilities required for any particular board appointment including that of the chairperson.
- identify sutiable candidates to fill vacancies when they arise.
- recommendations regarding directors standing for reappointments
- be seen to operate independently for the benefit of shareholders.

Remuneration committee

The role of the remuneration committee – to have an appropriate reward policy that attracts, retains and motivates directors to achieve the long-term interests of shareholders.

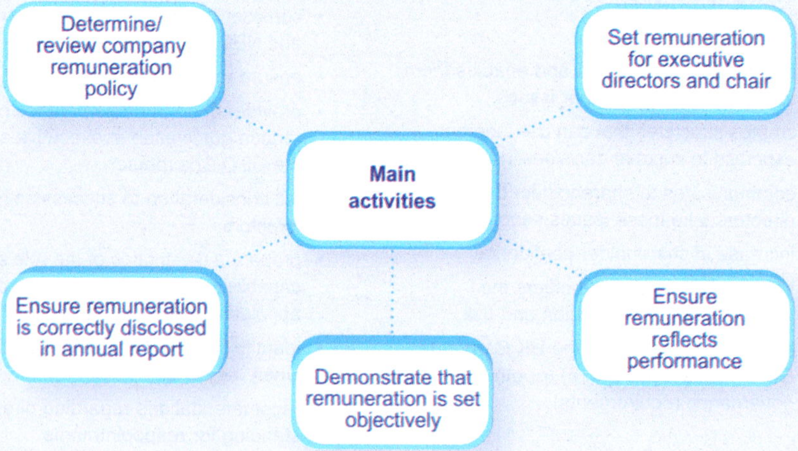

Responsibilities of the remuneration committee

- determine and regularly review the framework, board policy and specific terms for the remuneration, terms and conditions of employment of the chairperson, board and executive directors – including design of targets and any bonus scheme payments
- recommend and monitor the level and structure of the remuneration of senior managers
- establish pension provision policy for all board members
- set detailed remuneration for all executive directors and the chairperson
- ensure that the executive directors and key management are fairly rewarded
- the remuneration of the executive directors and key management is set by individuals with no personal interest
- agree any compensation for loss of office of any executive director.

Components of directors' remuneration package

- Basic salary – e.g. based on the skills required to do the job, individual's performance and market rates
- Performance related – e.g. dependent on the achievement of performance measurement criteria
- Pension – only basic salary is pensionable
- Benefits in kind – e.g. non-wage compensations in addition to their normal wage and salaries

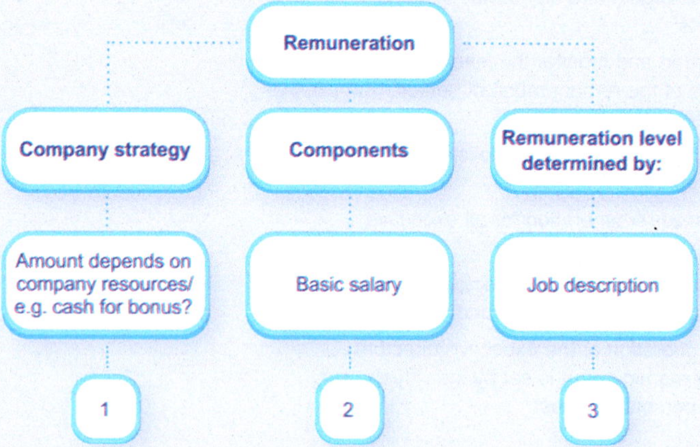

1

- Judge where to position remuneration compared to other companies
- Be aware of remuneration levels in comparable companies
- Be aware of pay and conditions throughout the company

2

- Performance related pay – linked to company success – short-term bonus – share options
- Pension contributions
- Benefits in kind

3

- Not too small – could lead to lack of motivation/ underachievement

  Not too easily earned to ensure that directors to improve performance
- Significant proportion based on performance related elements
- To attract and possibly motivate if increase with performance

Non-executive directors' remuneration

- NED remuneration consists of a basic salary and non-executive directors may receive share awards.
- Equity-based remuneration to non-executive directors should be fully vested on the grant date, but still subject to applicable holding periods.
- Performance measures remuneration whilst advocated in executive remuneration packages is not generally supported for non-executive remuneration.

Audit committee roles

- Most of the board objectives relating to internal controls will be delegated to the audit committee.
- Consists entirely of NEDs – one with recent financial experience.

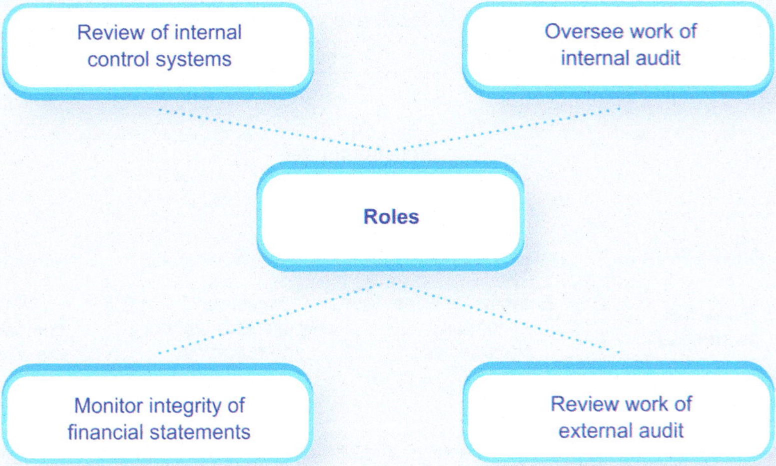

The role of the risk committee

Risk committee
Main aims: • Raise awareness of risk. • Ensure processes in place to identify, report and monitor risks. • Update company's risk profile.

- The committee will include both executive and non-executive directors, with the majority being NEDs.

chapter

9

Stakeholders and corporate social responsibility

In this chapter

- Social responsibility.
- 4 part model of CSR.
- Managing stakeholder relations.
- Institutional investors.
- Institutional shareholder intervention.
- Corporate citizenship.

Social responsibility

- Corporation is separate legal entity therefore has responsibilities to others.
- Corporate social responsiblity (CSR) refers to organisations considering and managing their impact on a variety of stakeholders.

CSR Strategy

A suggested approach to develop and pursue CSR strategy is as follows:

- The board, must make an authentic, firm, and public commitment to CSR.
- Determine the critical business objectives and priorities of the company.
- Develop a CSR strategy that will contribute to the achievement of those objectives.
- Integrate CSR into the culture, governance and strategy development of the company.

4 part model of CSR

Carroll's model of CSR has 4 increasing levels. True CSR satisfies all 4.

Responsibility	Explanation
Economic	• Business being financially sustainable. • Shareholders want reasonable returns, staff want fair wages, customers want value etc.
Legal	• Operate within the boundaries of the law. • Follow regulations and legal requirements.
Ethical	• Go beyond legal obligations. • Focus on doing what is right, just, and fair.
Philanthropic	• Voluntary actions to improve the quality of life for employees, communities, and society at large. • E.g. charitable donations, community service, and other initiatives that promote social welfare.

Developing a CSR strategy

Managing stakeholder relations

Mendelow's stakeholder mapping matrix

- Classifies stakeholders according to their level of power and interest in the organisation.
- Matrix used to determine company's action regarding each group.
- Company focus on key players, then those to keep satisfied to ensure they do not become key players.

Institutional investors

Institutional investors manage funds invested by individuals.

In the UK there are four types of institutional investor:

- pension funds
- life assurance companies
- unit trust
- investment trusts.

Institutional shareholder intervention

- Strategy: in terms of products sold, markets serviced, expansion pursued or any other aspect of strategic positioning.
- Operational performance: in terms of divisions that have persistently under-performed.
- Acquisitions and disposals: this might be in terms of executive decisions that have been inadequately challenged by NEDs.
- Remuneration policy: this might relate to a failure of the remuneration committee to curtail extreme or self-serving executive rewards.
- Internal controls: failure in health and safety, quality control, budgetary control or IT projects.
- Succession planning: a failure to adequately balance board composition or recommendation of replacement executives without adequate consideration
- Social responsibility: a failure to adequatel protect or respond to instances of environmental contamination or other areas of public concern.

Corporate citizenship

The organisation as a corporate citizen

Corporate citizen = expanded view of corporation in society. Implies corporate accountability.

Corporate accountability = whether the organisation is in some way answerable for the consequences of its actions beyond its relationship with shareholders.

Reasons for viewing company as corporate citizen

Government failure

- Government may be too slow to legislate against risks with new products and services.
- Other influences e.g. lack of political will, actions of pressure groups etc. also impede government action.
- Company must therefore take responsibility for safety of products/services.

Corporate power

- Over time, companies have tended to gain more power.
- E.g. decisions on where to locate workforce, privatisation of 'old' state monopolies.
- Companies should therefore use that power responsibly.

chapter

10

Effective leadership

In this chapter

- The nature and importance of leadership.
- What makes an effective leader?
- Leadership and management.
- Leadership and culture.
- Influence of culture.
- Entre and Intrapreneurship.

The nature and importance of leadership

- Buchanan and Huczynski define a leader as 'someone who exercises influence over other people'.
- Another definition is: Leadership is an interpersonal influence directed toward the achievement of a goal or goals.

Three important parts of this definition are the terms interpersonal, influence, and goal:

- Interpersonal – means between persons. Thus, a leader has more than one person (group) to lead.
- Influence – is the power to affect others.
- Goal – is the end one strives to attain.

Basically, this traditional definition of leadership says that a leader influences more than one person towards a goal.

Leadership can be viewed from three standpoints

- an attribute or a position, e.g. the managing director
- a characteristic of a person – a natural leader
- a category of behaviour.

What makes an effective leader?

Trait theories

Many great leaders were considered to have:

- physical traits, such as drive, energy, appearance and height
- personality traits, such as adaptability, enthusiasm and self-confidence
- social traits, such as co-operation, tact, courtesy and administrative ability.

Problems with trait theories:

- There will always be counter arguments – one theorist will say a leader should always be courteous whereas another will say that a rude and effective leader was identified.

Behavioural/style theories

- The essence of leadership style theories is that a successful leader will exhibit a pattern of behaviour (i.e. 'style') in gaining the confidence of those they wish to lead.

There are four main management styles:

- Tells (autocratic) – the manager makes all the decisions and issues instructions which are to be obeyed without question.
- Sells (persuasive) – the manager still makes all the decisions, but believes that team members must be motivated to accept them in order to carry them out properly.
- Consults (participative) – the manager confers with the team and takes their views into account, although still retains the final say.
- Joins (democratic) – the leader and the team members make the decision together on the basis of consensus.

Problems with behavioural theories:

- Unfortunately, as with trait theories, it is possible to find counter examples.

Contingency/contextual theories

- The modern consensus is that there is no one best style of leadership that is equally effective for all circumstances.
- A theory that is a mixture of both trait and contingency is the situational approach.

Leadership and management

- **A leader can be a manager, but a manager is not necessarily a leader.**
- Management is the process of setting and achieving the goals of the organisation through the functions of management: planning, organising, directing (or leading), and controlling.
- Leadership deals with the interpersonal aspects of a manager's job, whereas planning, organising, and controlling deal with the administrative aspects.
- Differentiating between leadership and management - employees willingly follow leaders because they want to, not because they have to.

Leadership and culture

It has been proposed that there are two types of leaders:

- Transactional leaders tend to be more passive. They see their relationship with their followers in terms of a trade.
- Transformational leaders more proactive. They see their role as inspiring and motivating others to work at levels beyond mere compliance.
- Only transformational leadership is said to be able to change team/organisational cultures and move them in a new direction.
- Transformational leadership enhances the motivation, morale, and job performance of followers.

NB The distinguishing feature of transformational leadership is the ability to bring about significant change.

Influence of culture

The Cultural Web

- Stories
- Routines and rituals
- Organisational structures
- Control systems
- Power structures
- Symbols

Advantages of strong culture:

- facilitate good communication
- social identity and a sense of belonging
- strengthen the dominant values and attitudes
- affect the organisation's strategy and ability to respond to change.

Disadvantages of strong culture:

A strong culture that does not have positive attributes in relation to stakeholders and change is a hindrance to effectiveness.

- difficult to change
- affect the organisation's ability or desire to learn new skills
- may stress inappropriate values
- culture clash e.g. in a merger
- not be attuned to the environment.

Entre and Intrapreneurship

- An **entrepreneur** is an individual that 'starts-up' a business, is the owner and take all of the risk of financial loss.
- An **intrapreneur** is an employee of the company and does not usually have any ownership and minimum risk of financial loss.

Talent management

Talent management is all about recruiting, retaining and developing high quality employees.

chapter

11

Reporting to stakeholders

In this chapter

- Disclosure – general principles.
- Sustainability.
- Social and environmental reporting.
- Benefits and drawbacks of social and environmental reporting.
- Integrated reporting.
- Objectives for integrated reporting.
- How to prepare an integrated report.
- Value creation process.

Disclosure – general principles

- The AGM is seen as the most important, and perhaps only, opportunity for the directors to communicate with the shareholders of the company.
- As the only legally-required disclosure to shareholders, the annual report and accounts are often the only information shareholders receive from the company.
- General principles of disclosure relate to the need to create and maintain communication channels with shareholders and other stakeholders. This disclosure becomes the mechanism through which governance is given transparency.
- Principles of mandatory disclosure discuss the target for disclosure (particularly shareholders) and the mechanism for disclosure (e.g. annual report or meetings).

NB Improvements in disclosure result in better transparency, which is the most important aim of governance reform worldwide.

Sustainability

- **Sustainable development** is development that meets the needs of the present without compromising the ability of future generations.

Environmental footprint – an attempt to evaluate the size of a company's impact on the environment in three respects:

- company's resource consumption
- harm to the environment brought about by pollution emissions
- measurement of the resource consumption and pollution emissions in terms of harm to the environment in either qualitative, quantitative or replacement terms.

Social footprint – evaluates sustainability in three areas of capital

- Human Capital – personal health, knowledge, skills, experience that individuals have and use to take effective action.
- Social Capital – networks of people and the mutually-held knowledge and skills they have and use in order to take effective action.
- Constructed Capital – material things, such as tools, technologies, roads, utilities, infrastructures, etc., that people produce and use in order to take effective action.

Sustainability Audit

A sustainability audit is an in depth examination of an organisation's entire environmental management system and associated arrangements.

Social and environmental reporting

Environmental reporting

- The 'disclosure of information on environment related issues and performance by an entity'.

It typically contains details of environmental performance in areas such as:

- measures of emissions (e.g. pollution, waste and greenhouse gases)
- consumption (e.g. of energy, water and non-renewable mineral deposits).

Social reporting

Social reporting is generally context specific, and typical contents will vary with industry. For example, the following issues should be included in a company's considerations:

- human rights issues
- work place, occupational health and safety
- training and employee issues
- fair pay for employees and suppliers
- fair business practices minority and equity issues.

Benefits and drawbacks of social and environmental reporting

Benefits	Drawbacks
Increasingly important to investors in investment decision	Additional cost of reporting systems
Reporting makes companies aware of potential risk to reputation	Ambiguity of measures used
Employees use this detail in choosing employers	
Influences customer buying decision	
Pre-empts potential regulatory intervention	
Promotes attention to good corporate governance	
Positive impact on share price	
Transparency of information	

Integrated reporting (<IR>)

Integrated reporting

Integrated Reporting demonstrates the linkages between an organisation's strategy, governance and financial performance and the social, environmental and economic context within which it operates.

Integrated Reporting can help business to take more sustainable decisions and enable investors and other stakeholders to understand how an organisation is really performing.

An Integrated Report should be a single report which is the organisation's primary report in most jurisdictions the Annual Report or equivalent.

Central to Integrated Reporting is the challenge facing organisations to create and sustain value inthe short, medium and longer term.

An integrated report is a concise communication about how an organisation's strategy, governance, performance and prospects, in the context of its external environment, lead to the creation of value in the short, medium and long term.

Objectives for integrated reporting:

- To improve the quality of information available to providers of financial capital.
- To provide a more cohesive and efficient approach to corporate reporting that draws on different reporting strands and communicates the full range of activities.
- To enhance accountability and stewardship for the broad base of capitals (financial, manufactured, intellectual, human, social and relationship, and natural.
- To support integrated thinking, decision making and actions that focus on the creation of value over the short, medium and long term.

Five other types of sustainable capital

These are:

Manufactured capital
Material goods, or fixed assets which contribute to the production process rather than being the output itself – e.g. tools, machines and buildings.

Intellectual capital
This form of capital can be described as the value of a company or organisation's employee knowledge, business training and any proprietary information that may provide the company with a competitive advantage.

(NB: Some of the subsets of intellectual capital include human capital, information capital, brand awareness and instructional capital.)

Human capital
This can be described as consisting of people's health, knowledge, skills and motivation. Enhancing human capital through education and training is central.

Social capital
This can be described as being concerned with the institutions that help us maintain and develop human capital in partnership with others; e.g. families, communities, businesses.

Natural capital
This can be described as any stock or flow of energy and material within the environment that produces goods and services e.g. climate regulation, climate change, CO2 emissions.

How to prepare an integrated report

The following seven guiding principles underpin the preparation:

- Strategic focus and future orientation – highlighting significant risks, opportunities and dependencies flowing from the organisation's market position and business model, and giving the management's view of how the organisation balances short, medium and long term interests.
- Connectivity of information – show a holistic picture of the combination, inter-relatedness and dependencies between the factors that affect the organisation's ability to create value over time.
- Stakeholder relationships – should provide insight into the nature and quality of the organisation's relationships with its key stakeholders.
- Materiality – Identifying relevant matters based on their ability to affect value creation.
- Conciseness – should give sufficient context to understand the organisation's strategy, governance and prospects without being burdened by less relevant information.
- Reliability and completeness – should include all material matters, both positive and negative, in a balanced way and without material error.

Value creation process

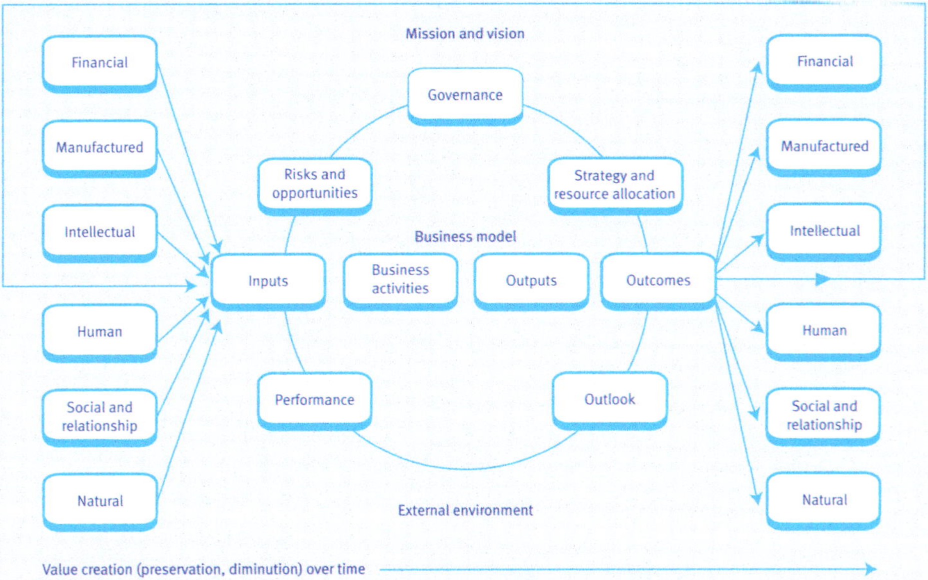

chapter

12

Management internal control systems and reporting

In this chapter

- Internal control roles and responsibilities.
- Internal control objectives and benefits.
- Sound control systems.
- Roles and responsibilities in risk management and internal control.
- Effective internal control systems.
- Information flows for management.
- Information characteristics and quality.
- Fraud risk management strategy.

Internal control roles and responsibilities

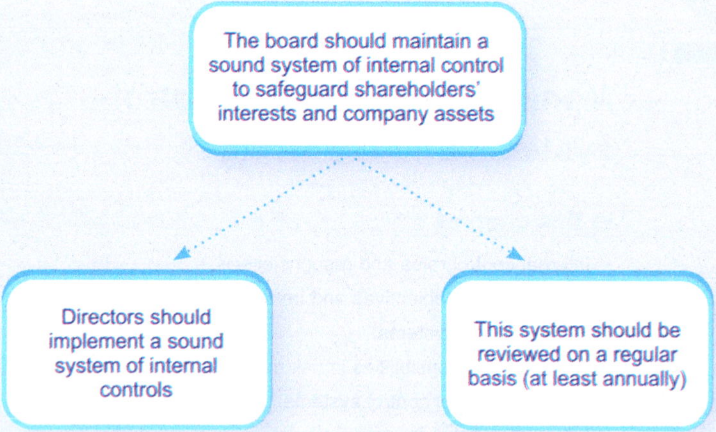

Internal control objectives and benefits

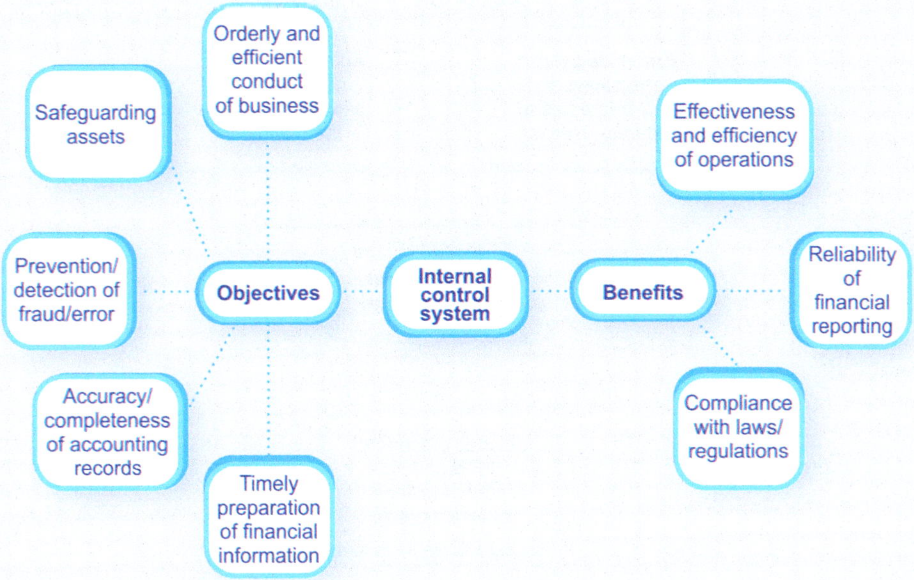

Sound control systems

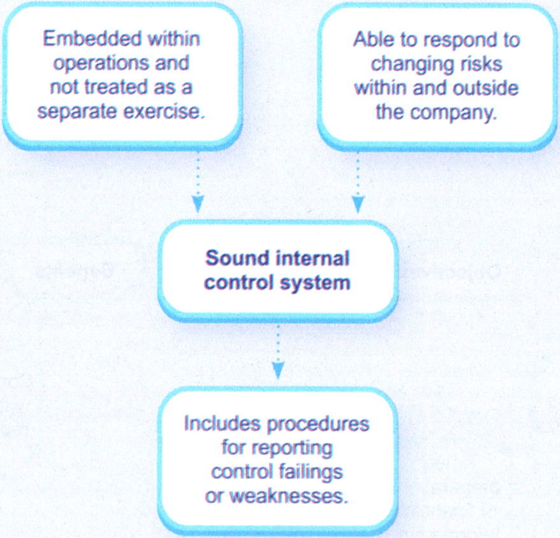

Roles and responsibilities in risk management and internal control

Many stakeholders involved – not just directors.

Role / Responsibility

CEO

Ultimate responsibility for internal control system

Board of directors

- Ensuring adequac and effectiveness of internal control system
- Set corporate governance policy

Risk committee

Assists board in risk management obligations

Executive management

Setting internal control policies, and monitoring effectiveness of those systems

Role / Responsibility

Internal auditors

- Evaluate the effectiveness of internal controls
- Recommend improvements

Heads of business units

Establish specific internal control procedures and policies for their units

All employees

Operating and adhering to internal control procedures

External auditors

Advice on establishing and monitoring internal controls

Effective internal control systems

Elements of an effective internal control system

1 Control environment

- 'Tone at the top' or the ethics and culture of the organisation. Set by management philosophy and style

2 Risk assessment

- Set objectives of organisation
- Then for each objective, identify and assess the risks affecting that objective
- Consider internal and external risks
- Distinguish between controllable and uncontrollable risks

3 Control activities

- Policies and procedures ensuring decisions and instructions of management carried out
- Occur at all levels in an organisation

4 Monitoring

- Control system must be monitored – normally by internal audit

5 Information & communication

- Communicate correct information to correct people so they can carry out their responsibilities
- Need quality information systems providing internal and external information

Information flows for management

Three management levels recognised in company.

Each level has responsibilities for internal controls and risk.

Information systems available to provide required information for each level.

Management level	Activity	Internal control responsibilities	Risk responsibilities
Strategic	Monitoring and controlling organisation as a whole	Reviewing internal control systems to ensure they are effective	Assess the risk outcomes of different decisions – also advised by the risk committee
1	2	3	4

Information flows for management – (continued)

1	2	3	4
Tactical	Implement decisions of strategic managers: ensure departments operating correctly	Establish control systems, remedy control weaknesses, inform strategic management of control weaknesses	Advise strategic managers on risks identified receive reports on operational risks and recommend risk mitigation procedures
Operational	Controlling day-to-day operations of the organisation	Operation of detailed internal controls – report weaknesses to tactical managers	Identify risks at operational level and inform tactical managers

Information characteristics and quality

Characteristic	Strategic	→	Operational
Time period	Forecast	→	Historical
Timeliness	Delayed	→	Immediately available
Objectivity	Subjective	→	Objective
Quantifiability	Qualitative	→	Quantitative
Accuracy	Approximate	→	Accurate
Certainty	Uncertain	→	Certain
Completeness	Partial	→	Complete
Breadth	Broad	→	Specific
Detail	Little detail	→	Highly detailed

Fraud risk management strategy

A risk management strategy needs to be developed for fraud.

This strategy should include three key elements:

- Fraud prevention

  For example:

  – An anti-fraud culture
  – Risk awareness
  – Whistleblowing
  – Sound internal control systems

- Fraud detection

  For example: performing regular checks, e.g. stocktaking and cash counts.

- Fraud response

  For example: Dealing with suspected cases of fraud, theft or corruption via procedures for evidence-gathering to assist decision making and subsequently admissible in any legal action.

Organisations response to fraud may include:

- Internal disciplinary action, in accordance with personnel policies.
- Civil litigation for the recovery of loss.
- Criminal prosecution through the police.

chapter

13

Audit and compliance

In this chapter

- Function and importance of internal audit.
- Factors affecting the need for internal audit.
- Auditor independence.
- Potential ethical threats.
- Audit committee internal controls.
- Audit committee and internal audit.
- Audit committee and external auditors.
- Reporting on internal controls to shareholders.

Function and importance of internal audit

Exam focus

Internal audit = an independent appraisal activity established within an organisation as a service to it.

Main roles/functions of internal audit:

Factors affecting the need for internal audit

Auditor independence

Internal auditor independence necessary to ensure work carried out objectively.

Factors protecting independence

- Internal auditor independent of executive management.
- Chief internal auditor reports to audit committee.
- Chief internal auditor has access to Chairperson.
- Audit committee approve appointment and termination of chief internal auditor.

Potential ethical threats

= threats (real or perceived) to ability of auditor to provide independent opinion.

Apply to both internal and external audit.

Audit committee and internal controls

Audit committee and internal audit

Audit committee responsible for overseeing work of internal audit function.

Audit committee and external auditors

Audit committee responsible for oversight of company relations with external auditors.

The UK Corporate Governance Code provides recommendations regarding the work of audit committee and company's external auditors:

Reporting on internal controls to shareholders

Important points regarding reporting to shareholders:

Audit committee and shareholders

- Chair of audit committee available at AGM for shareholder questions
- Shareholders right to know whether internal controls sufficient to safeguard their investment
- Sarbanes Oxley more detailed legal reporting requirements
- Annual report explains work of audit committee
- To provide shareholders with necessary information board should conduct an annual review of internal control systems
- Review covers all material controls and risk management systems

chapter

14

Risk management

In this chapter

- Risk definition.
- Why incur and manage risk?
- The role of the Board in risk management.
- Risk management.
- Enterprise risk management.
- COSO ERM framework matrix.
- Risk identification: Strategic and operational risks.
- Risk identification: Business risks.
- Risk assessment.
- Risk heat map.
- Risk management strategies.
- Risk monitoring.
- Embedding risk.
- Embedding risk in systems.
- Embedding risk in culture.

Risk definition

- Risk can be defined as an unrealised future loss arising from a present action or inaction.
- Risks are the opportunities and dangers associated with uncertain future events.

Why incur and manage risk?

Why incur risk?

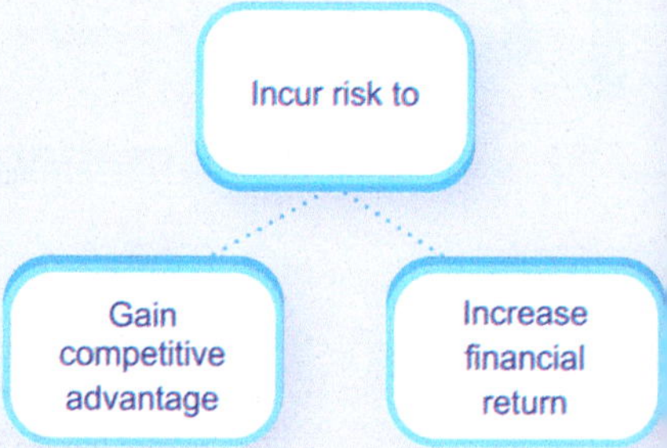

Why manage risk?

- Downside risks managed to identify new risks and changes in existing risks.
- Upside risks identified to make best use of opportunities.

The role of the board in risk management

Main role

- Considering risk at strategic level and defining organisation's appetite and approach to risk.

Other roles

- Setting risk appetite in terms of attitude and capacity.
- Communicating risk strategy to company.
- Monitoring risk management plans.
- Determining residual risk based on cost-benefit approach.

Framework for board consideration of risk

Risk management

Risk management

Risk management = process of reducing adverse consequences by reducing likelihood of event or its impact.

- Responsibility for risk management system rests with management.

Enterprise risk management (ERM)

Principles of (ERM)

- risk management in the context of business strategy
- risk management is everyone's responsibility, with the tone set from the top
- the creation of a risk aware culture
- a comprehensive and holistic approach to risk management
- consideration of a broad range of risks (strategic, financial, operational and compliance)
- a focused risk management strategy, led by the board (embedding risk within an organisation's culture).

COSO ERM framework matrix

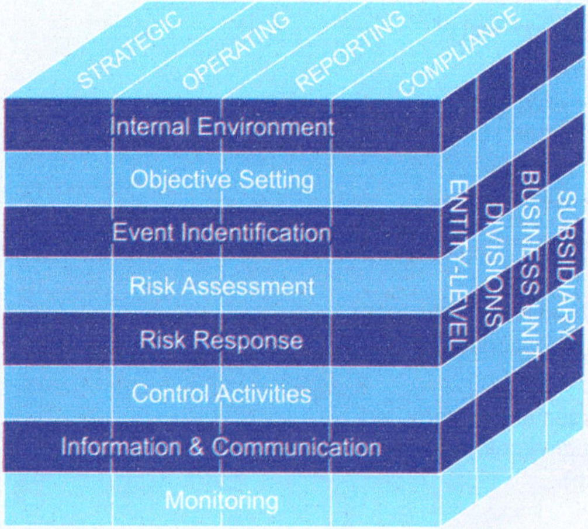

Risk identification: Strategic and operational risks

Strategic risks	Operational risks
Risks arising from consequences of strategic decisions	Losses arising from business operations
Arise from strategic positioning of company in its environment	Arise from inadequate or failed internal processes
Risks include not enhancing old products and producing 'incorrect' new products	Risks include fraud, quality control failures and lack of production
Identified and assessed at senior management level. Managed by risk management strategy	Identified at operational level. Managed by internal control systems

Risk identification: Business risks

Definition

Business risks are strategic risks that threaten the health and survival of the whole business.

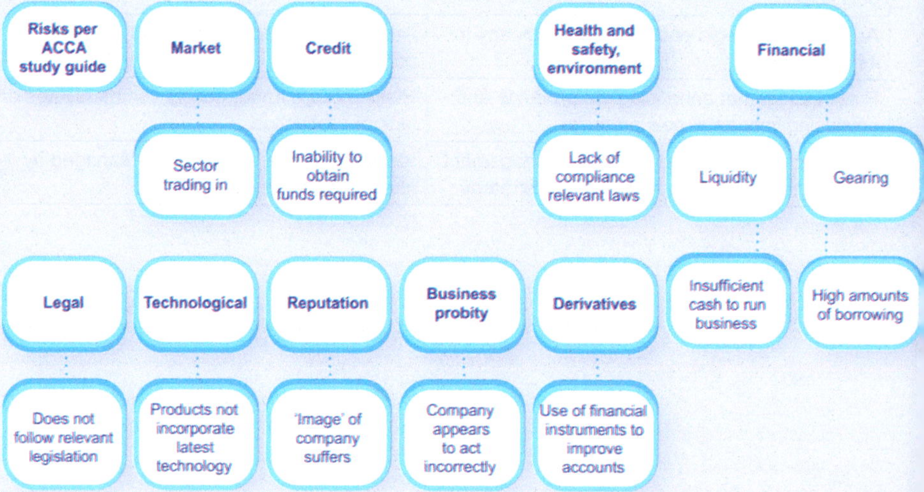

Risk assessment

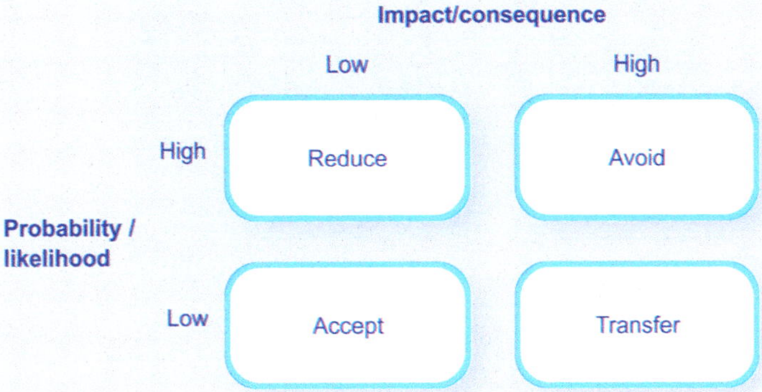

Risk heat map

Potential Impact	Remote	Unlikely	Possible	Likely	Probable
Extreme	5	10	15	20	25
High	4	8	12	16	20
Medium	3	6	9	12	15
Low	2	4	6	8	10
Negligiable	1	2	3	4	5
Likelihood					
% ranges	0-10%	>10-25%	>25-50%	>50-90%	>90-100%

Risk management strategies

- Strategies for managing risk – TARA

Transference (or sharing)	Transfer risk to third party e.g. use of insurance
Avoidance	Risk decreased to zero by avoiding risky areas e.g. withdrawing from business area. However, risk may be unavoidable – so strategy has limited use
Reduction	Limit exposure to risk or decrease effects of risk should it crystallise
Acceptance	Accept risk may occur and choose to deal with consequences of risk if it does occur. Used where adverse impact of risk is minimal

Further risk management strategies

- Risk avoidance = risk literally avoided.
- Risk retention = risk retained within organisation.

Diversifying/spreading risk

- Aim to reduce total risk.
- Can diversify operations
  - make different products or invest in different countries.
- Works best where returns are negatively correlated.

The As Low As Reasonably Practicable Principle (ALARP)

- Expresses a point at which the cost of additional risk reduction would be grossly disproportionate to the benefits achieved.
- Usually applied to safety critical, high integrity systems e.g. oil rig.

Risk monitoring

Risk auditing

- = provision of independent view of risks and controls in organisation
- May be obligatory (e.g. Sarbanes-Oxley)
- Carried out by internal and/or external audit teams.

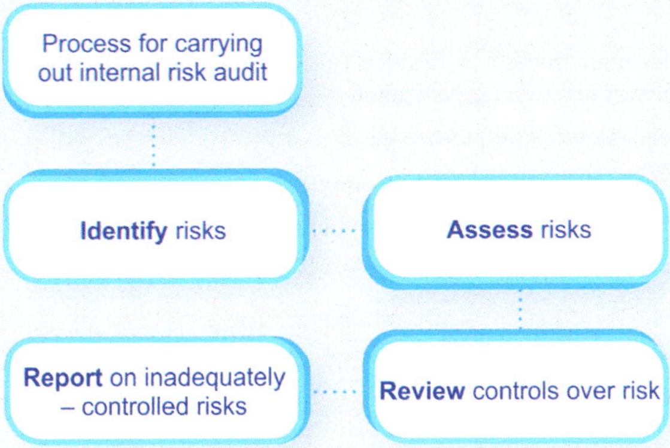

Embedding risk

- The aim of embedding risk management is to ensure that it is 'part of the way we do business'

Considered at two levels:

- embedding risk in systems

Embedding risk in systems

- = ensuring risk management is included within control systems of an organisation
- Not a separate system – part of overall control system
- May be statutory requirement (USA) or code of practice (UK)

Process of embedding risk:

1. Identify controls already operating in organisation
2. Monitor controls to ensure they work
3. Improve/refine controls as required
4. Document how controls recorded and tested (e.g. performance metrics)

Embedding risk in culture

- Risk awareness is a capability of an organisation to be able to recognise risks when they arise, from whatever source they may come.

Embedding risk awareness

- Risk management being considered 'normal' for organisation therefore all employees follow risk management policies.
- Risk management culture starts at 'top' of company – provides open culture/better risk management.

chapter

15

Professionalism, ethical codes and the public interest

In this chapter

- Profession and professionalism.
- The public interest.
- Accountants and the public interest – role and influence.
- Corporate codes of ethics.
- Professional codes of ethics.
- Benefits and drawbacks of corporate and professional code of ethics.
- Ethical threats and safeguards.
- Bribery and corruption.
- Ethical conflict.
- Issue and context related factors.

Profession and professionalism

Profession

Definition

- A body of theory and knowlege which is used to support the public interest.

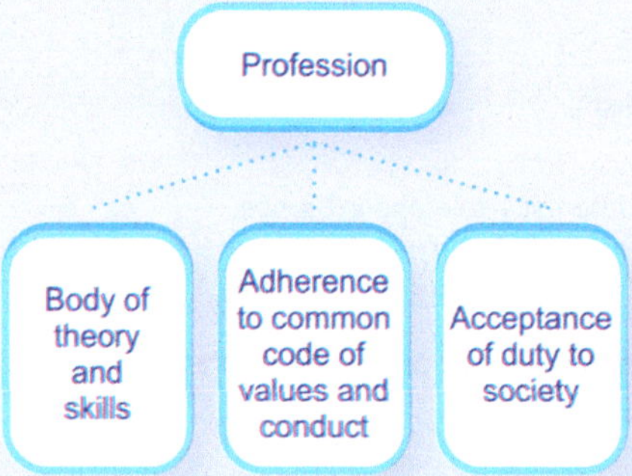

Professionalism

Definition

- Taking action to support the public interest.
- Acting professionally.

Views of professionalism

Reactive – noting negative aspects of accounting and taking action to remove those aspects e.g. legislation post Enron.

Proactive – seeking out new ways for accounting to support the public interest e.g. self-imposed codes of conduct.

The public interest

Definition

That which supports the good of society as a whole (as opposed to what serves the interests of individual members of society or of specific sectional interest groups).

- Ethical codes confirm that acting against the public interest is not appropriate for an accountant.
- When considering whether to disclose information or not the accountant will need to evaluate each situation on its merits.

Responsible leadership

Recent research has identified the following attributes for leaders that are important to demonstrate responsible leadership.

- The ability to make informed ethical judgments
- Displaying moral courage and aspiring to positive change
- A business leader requires a forward-looking rather than a backward-looking responsibility orientation
- Engaging in long-term thinking and in perspective-taking
- Communicating effectively with stakeholders
- Participating in collective problem-solving

Accountants and the public interest – role and influence

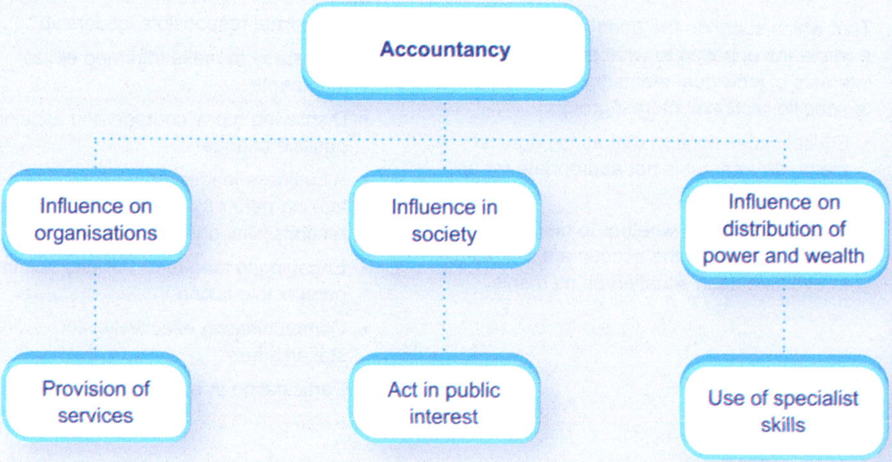

Corporate code of ethics

Definition

= application of ethical values to business behaviour.

How business ethics affects stakeholders

Shareholders

Expect fair and proper return on their investment.

Company should provide this return and information on how shareholders investment managed

Suppliers

Suppliers attempt to provide quality goods on time.

Company should pay invoices promptly, select suppliers on known criteria e.g. 'fair trade' principles

Wider community

Company affects society as a whole. CSR report explains how company treats wider community

Business values

Mission statement mentions

- products/services provided
- financial objectives
- role of business in society

Employees

How business relates to employees.

Company recognises employee rights in areas such as working conditions, training, health and safety

Customer relations

Company has responsibility to produce quality goods/ services at reasonable price

Professional code of ethics

Fundamental ethical principles

Integrity
Members should be straightforward and honest in all professional/business relationships

Objectivity
Members do not allow bias or conflict of interest in business judgements

Competence
Duty to maintain professional knowledge and skill at appropriate level

Confidentiality
Information on clients not disclosed without appropriate specific authority

Professional behaviour
Members must comply with relevant laws and avoid actions discrediting the profession

Benefits and drawbacks of corporate and professional code of ethics

Benefits		Drawbacks
Provides framework for conflict resolution		It is only a code – may not fit the precise ethical issue
Provides guidelines for similar ethical disputes and methods of resolution		Can be interpreted in different ways which may appear ethically incorrect to two different people
Provides boundaries across which it is ethically incorrect to pass		May be no clear or effective punishment for breaching the code

Ethical theats and safeguards

Ethical threats and safeguards

Threats = situation where person tempted not to follow code of ethics

Safeguards = guidance or course of action aimed at reducing or eliminating threats

Main safeguards include:

Profession	Work environment	Individual
• Education and training • CPD • Monitoring of work • Disciplinary proceedings	• Internal control systems • Review procedures • Codes of ethics • Disciplinary procedures	• Compliance with standards • Mentoring • Recording contentious issues • Assistance from professional body

Bribery and corruption

- Corruption is bribery and any other behaviour in relation to persons entrusted with responsibilities in the public or private sector which violates their duties and is aimed at obtaining undue advantages of any kind for themselves or for others.

Corruption and bribery

- Examples:
  - excessive 'hospitality'
  - facilitation payments
- it increases risk
- it is inherently unethical.

Relevant legislation

UK Bribery Act (2010)

- 4 offences
  - Offering, promising or giving bribe.
  - Requesting, agreeing to receive or accepting a bribe.
  - Bribing a foreign public official.
  - A corporate offence of failing to prevent bribery.

Ethical conflict

Factors to take into account in dealing with ethical conflict:

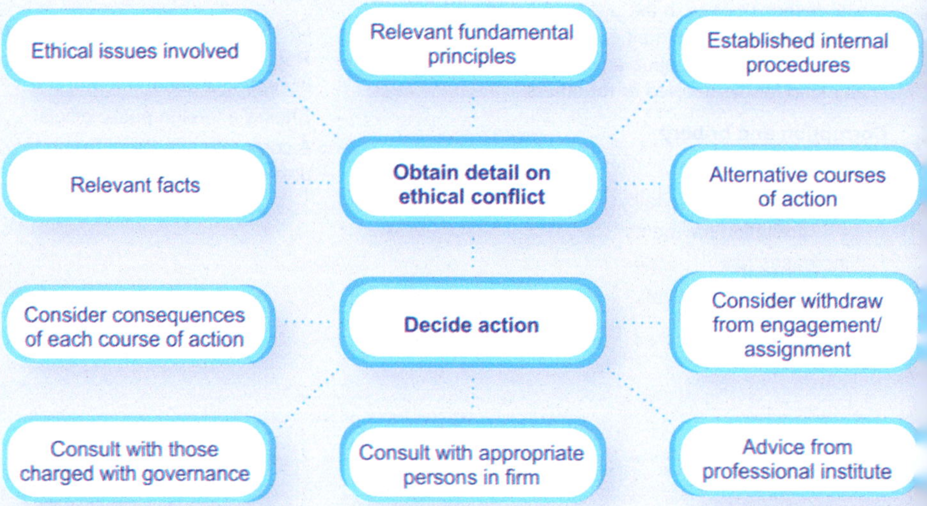

Issue and context related factors

Ability to make ethical decision depends on:

- issue related factors – how important decision is to decision-maker – factors affect moral intensity and moral framing.
- context-related factors – how factors relating to issue are viewed.

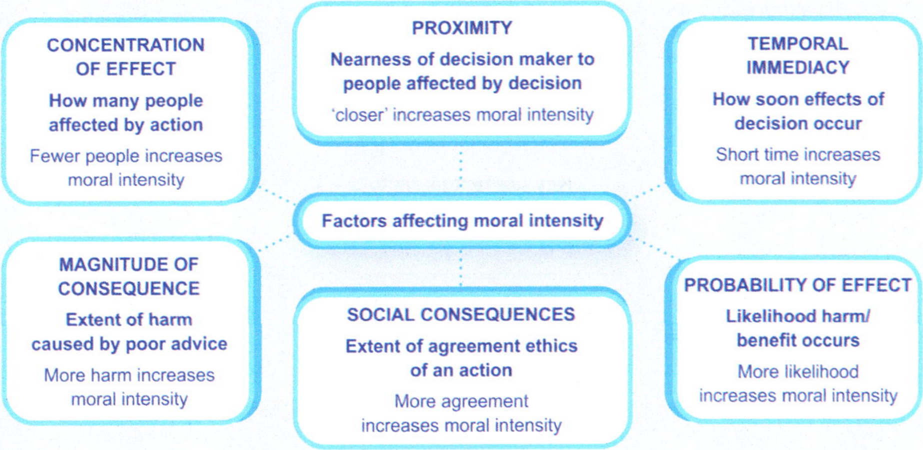

Context-related factors:

- behaviour rewarded by superiors – even though dubious – will it be continued.
- co-workers take same action – will it be continued.

Key contextual factors

- **System of reward** – Rewards based on achievement may encourage unethical decisions
- **Authority** – Senior manager unethical means junior likely to be also
- **Bureaucracy** – Follow rules – not normally consider ethics of decisions made
- **Cultural context** – Cultures have different ideas of 'ethics'
- **Group norms** – Follow what peer-group think is ethical
- **Work roles** – Provides ethical context e.g. accountants normally behave ethically

chapter

16

Organising for success

In this chapter

- The link between structure and strategy.
- Main structural types.
- Mintzberg's building blocks.
- Boundaryless organisations.
- Business process outsourcing.
- Harmon's process strategy matrix.
- Business process redesign.

The link between structure and strategy

How structure changes as strategy changes

- More specialisation
- More specialists
- More levels of authority
- More bureaucracy

How structure can impact on strategy

- The degree of organisational flexibility
- The level of specialist skills and associated decision making
- The degree of innovation and knowledge management
- Developing and supporting CSFs
- The degree of market focus

Main structural types

Types of structure

Entrepreneurial

- structure is built around the owner manager

Functional

- groups together employees that undertake similar task

Divisional

- splits organisation into several divisions
- either product based or geographical based

Matrix

- a combination of a functional and a divisional structure

Small organisation ← → Large organisation

Mintzberg's building blocks

As the business and its structure grows, different building blocks develop and can become more important:

Building block	What they want	What they provide	Structure in which they dominate
Strategic apex	Direction	Supervision	Simple
Technostructure	Efficiency	Procedures and standards	Machine bureaucracy
Operating core	Proficiency	Expertise and skills	Professional bureaucracy
Middle line	Concentration	Focus and control	Divisional
Support staff	Learning	Help and training	None

Boundaryless organisations

- The hollow structure – where non-core activities are outsourced.
- The modular structure – where some parts of product production are outsourced.
- The virtual structure – where the organisation is made up of a collaboration of other organisational parts.

Business process outsourcing

Advantages	Disadvantages
• Cost savings (currently the main decision-making factor). • Improved customer care. • Allows management to focus on core activities.	• Problems finding a single supplier for complex processes, resulting in fragmentation. • Firms are unwilling to outsource whole processes due to the strategic significance or security implications of certain elements. • Inflexible contracts and other problems managing suppliers. • Difficult to reverse and bring in-house again. • Problems measuring performance. • Data security.

Harmon's process strategy matrix

Strategic importance

Process complexity dynamics	Low	High
High	• Outsource	• Undertake process improvement
Low	• Use minimum resources	• Automate to gain efficiency
	Must be done but adds little value to products or services	Very important to success, high value added to products or services

Business process redesign

Typical causes of problems in processes

- activities are unnecessary
- activities are in the wrong order
- activities are in the wrong swim lane
- activities are missing
- activities take too long.

Typical solutions in processes

- removing swim lanes
- removing unnecessary activities
- combining job roles
- combining activities
- reducing handovers between swim lanes
- changing the order of activities
- outsourcing activities.

chapter

17

Technology in business

In this chapter

- IT - the strategic context.
- Types of e-businesses.
- Supply chain management (SCM).
- Upstream supply chain management.
- Downstream supply chain management.
- Disruptive technology.
- Artificial intelligence.
- Mobile (SMART) technology.
- Big Data.
- IT risks.
- IT controls.
- Promoting cyber security.
- Ethics of technology usage.
- Corporate digital responsibility (CDR).

IT – the strategic context

In the modern environment IT plays a role at all stages of the strategic planning process. For example,

- Strategic analysis: IT can help create business strengths or overcome existing weaknesses
- Strategic choice: IT can help create a competitive advantage or give access to new markets
- Strategic implementation: we've already seen how IT plays a role in BPR, for example.

Therefore we should consider IT at all stages of the syllabus. For example, we should incorporate IT influences within the PESTEL, 5 Forces, value chain etc.

Types of e-Business

Exchange initiated by	Delivery by: Business	Delivery by: Consumer
Business	B2B Business models, e.g. VerticalNet	B2C Business models, e.g. Amazon.com
Consumer	C2B Business models,e.g. Priceline.com	C2C Business models, e.g. eBay.com

Stages of e-business

1 Web presence

2 E-commerce

3 Integrated e-commerce

4 E-business

Benefits of e-business	Barriers to e-business
• Cost reduction	• Security concerns
• Increased revenue	• Set-up costs
• Better information for control	• Running costs
• Increased visibility	• Limited opportunities – type of business
• Enhanced customer service	• Limited resources
• Improved marketing	• Customer aversion
• Market penetration	
• Enhanced competitive advantage	

Supply chain management (SCM)

Supply chain management typically involves:

- re-organisation of processes
- greater use of IT systems
- providing more information to suppliers and customers
- more efficient inventory replenishment
- better co-ordination of new product development
- promotional activity integrated along the supply chain
- greater use of outsourcing.

Role of IT in SCM

- facilitated a move from push systems towards pull systems
- E-procurement has become a vital part of SCM
- facilitated better interaction with customers
- encouraged virtual integration.

Upstream supply chain management

E-procurement

Benefits	Risks
• Reduced labour costs • Lower inventories • Higher sales due to fewer inventory stock outs • Better control over product development • Greater choice of supplier • Better transaction history • Reduced admin	• Technology risks • Organisational risks – especially staff resistance • Costs savings fail to materialise • Requires new skills • It can be difficult to integrate different systems • Expensive to set up

Downstream supply chain management

Benefits	Problems
• Disintermediation • Tie-in • Continual updates • Differentiation • Two way communication • User communities • Better market research • Easier e-marketing • Reduced product failure rates • Customers can define specifications	• Relies on supplier willingness • Reaction of distributors/ retailers • Move to product orientation • Extra admin costs • Easily copied • Users must be representative • Become reactive rather than proactive • Can increase business risk and exit barriers

Disruptive technology

Advantages	Potential defences
• Better use of data • A frictionless customer experience • More personalisation of products/services • Lack of physical presence costs • Access to cheap capital	• Differentiating • Improving flexibility • Promoting physical presence • Take legal action • Relying on technophobia • Reacting sooner • Launch own disruptive tech

Artificial intelligence

AI – "a system's ability to correctly interpret external data, to learn from such data, and to use those learnings to achieve specific goals and tasks through flexible adaptation".

Artificial intelligence and finance

Examples include:

- using machine learning to code accounting entries and improve on the accuracy of rules-based approaches, enabling greater automation of processes
- improving fraud detection through more sophisticated, machine learning models of 'normal' activities and better prediction of fraudulent activities
- using machine learning-based predictive models to forecast revenues
- improving access to, and analysis of, unstructured data, such as contracts and emails.

Mobile (SMART) technology

All aspects of modern life are impacted by mobile technology, with major industries being completely transformed or new ones emerging, including:

- **Newspapers** – physical sales of newspapers in terminal decline
- **Advertising** – large scale mass advertising is in decline with a growth in smarter, targeted adverts
- **Music** e.g. Spotify
- **Banking** – the traditional high street branch continues to decline
- **Socialising** – social media
- **TV/Film** – Video streaming services such as **Netflix** and **Amazon Prime**

Big data

Characteristics of big data

- volume
- velocity
- variety

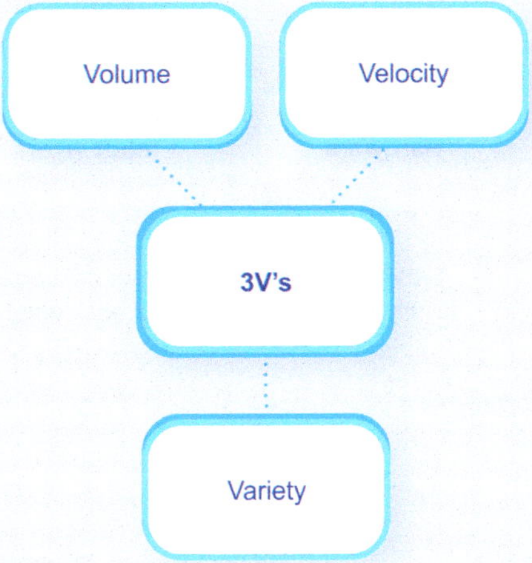

Strategic advantages from exploiting big data

- better knowledge of customers
- ability to spot trends earlier
- react before rivals
- proactively meet changing needs
- identify unsatisfied needs
- better market research and e-marketing
- better competitive advantages.

IT Risks

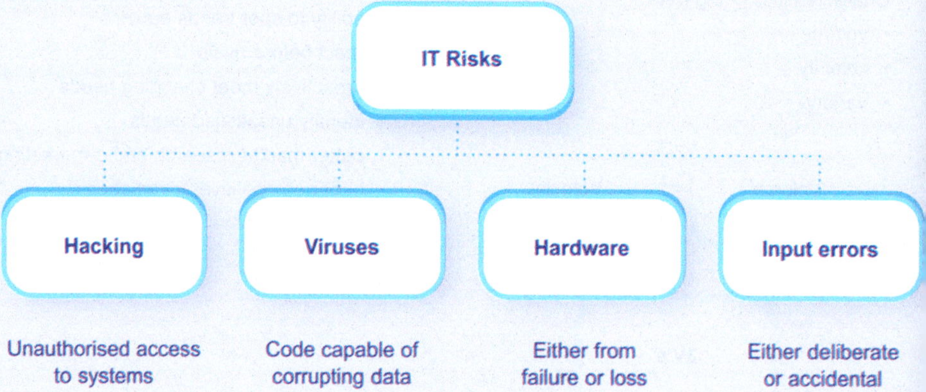
IT Risks
Hacking
Viruses
Hardware
Input errors
Unauthorised access to systems
Code capable of corrupting data
Either from failure or loss
Either deliberate or accidental

IT Controls

IT Controls

General

- personnel
- logical access
- access logging
- physical controls
- hardware security
- back-ups

Application

- authorisation
- pre-numbered forms
- control totals
- output checking

Software

- supplier selection
- retain original disks
- license checking

Network

- firewalls
- data encryption
- virus protection
- flow

Promoting cyber security

- Have a written policy.
- Provide ongoing training and assessment.
- Have a dedicated cyber security staff.
- Limit systems access.
- Limit data volume.
- Automate systems.

Ethics of technology usage

Legal considerations

GDPR
Data controllers

Ethical and social considerations

Ethical and social considerations are important for the following reasons:

- investor confidence
- customer confidence
- consumer safety
- attract employees
- sustainability
- stakeholder confidence
- risk pro-activity

Corporate digital responsibility (CDR)

The development of a **CDR strategy** is increasingly common in modern business and would include the following **5 key areas**:

- **Digital stewardship** – using data in a responsible and secure way
- **Customer expectations** – around data use and the need for transparency are increasing
- **Giving back** – e.g. a pharmaceutical company sharing clinical trial data with university researchers for no gain
- **Data value** – increasingly apparent to customers as well as businesses
- **Digital inclusion** – businesses need to be proactive to help and support users and reduce barriers and obstacles.

chapter

18

E-marketing

In this chapter

- Marketing mix (7P's).
- The 6I's.
- e-Branding.
- Using marketing in e-business.

Marketing mix (7P's)

Traditional marketing involves finding the correct mix of the following elements:

- Product.
- Price.
- Promotion.
- Place.

E-marketing expands this into three more areas:

- People.
- Physical evidence.
- Processes.

The 6I's

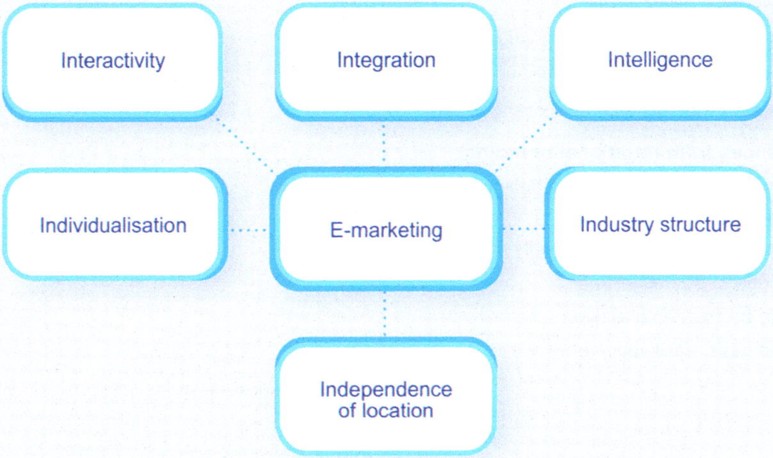
Interactivity
Integration
Intelligence
Individualisation
E-marketing
Industry structure
Independence of location

e-Branding

Potential e-branding strategies:

- match an existing brand
- modify an existing brand
- create a new brand
- form a partnership with an existing brand

Differences from traditional branding

- The information needs to be delivered in a more efficient manner
- It requires a more visual identity
- It needs to be easier to find
- It can be more interactive
- It can more easily evolve

Using marketing in e-business

Acquiring customers

- search engine marketing
- online PR
- online partnerships
- interactive adverts
- opt-in emails
- viral marketing
- evaluating online behaviour

Managing customers

Ensuring that customers keep returning to a website relies upon:

- tangibles
- reliability
- responsiveness
- assurance
- empathy

Empathy can be improved through:

- personalisation
- opt-in emails
- supporting online communities
- storing and using past transactions

chapter

19

Project management

In this chapter

- The project life cycle.
- The business case document.
- The project plan.
- The project initiation document.
- Key project staff.
- Project control.
- Project review.

The project life cycle

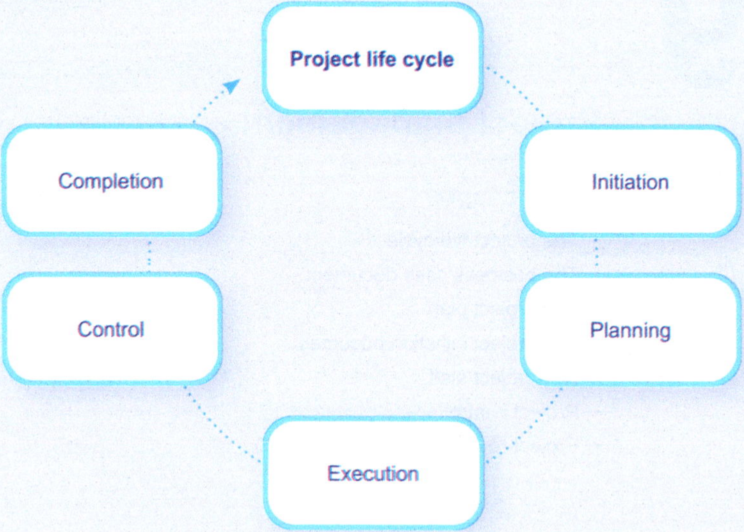

The business case document

Typical contents:	Reason:
• Strategic analysis	• Explains why project is needed
• Project benefits and costs	• Provides a financial rationale
• Project constraints	• Provides clear boundaries
• Risk analysis	• Managers can be more proactive to risks

Why have a formal document?

- to obtain funding for the project
- to compete with other projects for resources
- to improve planning
- to improve project management.

The project plan

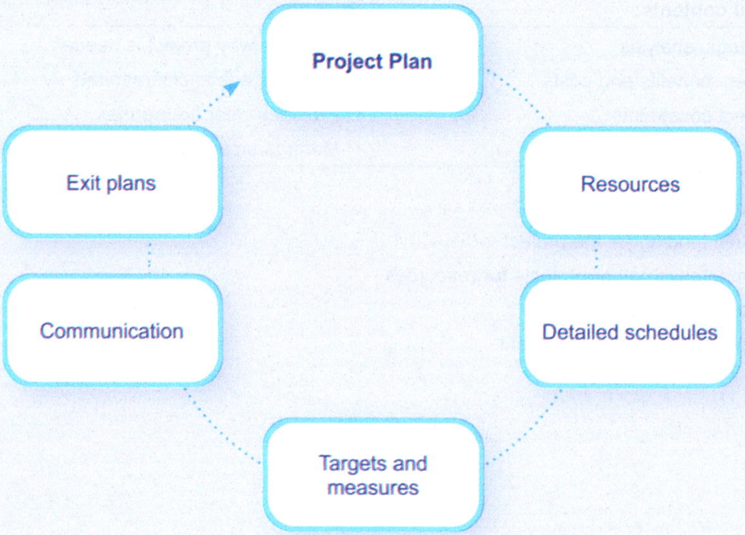

The project initiation document

What it contains	Benefits of having this
Clear responsibilities	Lines of authority for decision making Facilitates responsibility accounting
Detailed schedules	Clear path Improved efficiency
Targets and measures	Clear control points Early identification of problems
Exit plans	More efficient handover Easier exit for the project team

Key project staff

Project staff	Project roles
Project sponsor	Providing resources Approving changes Communicating organisational goals
Project manager	Building the business case Executing the plan Exercising control Managing team members
Team members	Make business and enabling changes Follow the plan

Project control

This has 3 stages:

- Create performance measures and targets
- Test performance at project gateways
- Take control actions if targets aren't met.

Potential control actions:

- Fast tracking
- Crashing
- Adding additional resources
- Scope reduction
- Adopting higher risk but potentially more efficient approaches
- Employee motivation.

Project review

Post project review (PPR) – reviews the performance of the project team.

Post implementation review (PIR) – reviews the output from the project.

Lessons learned (LL) – documents action points for similar projects in the future.

chapter

20

Financial decision making

In this chapter

- Options for raising equity finance.
- Options for raising debt finance.
- Other sources.
- Cost accounting.
- Break even analysis.
- Marginal decision making.
- Investment appraisal.
- Dealing with risk in decision making.
- Budgeting.
- Variance analysis.
- Other quantitative analysis techniques.

Options for raising equity finance

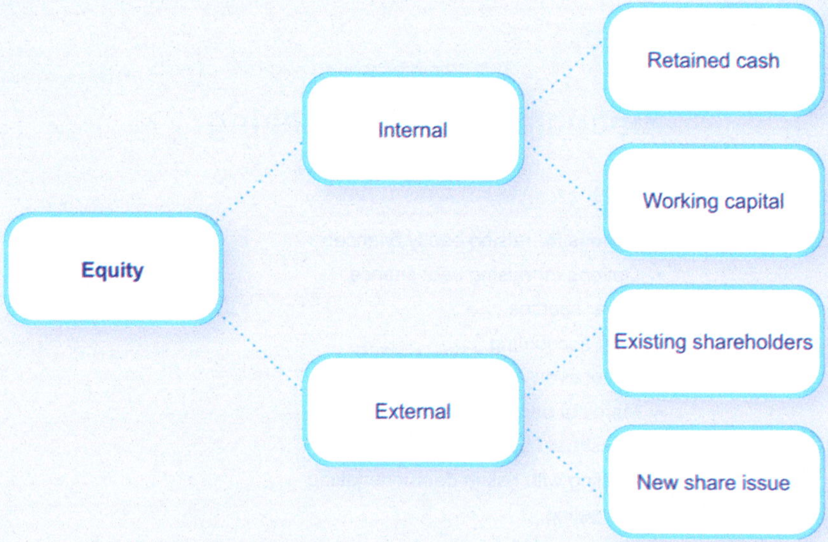

Options for raising debt finance

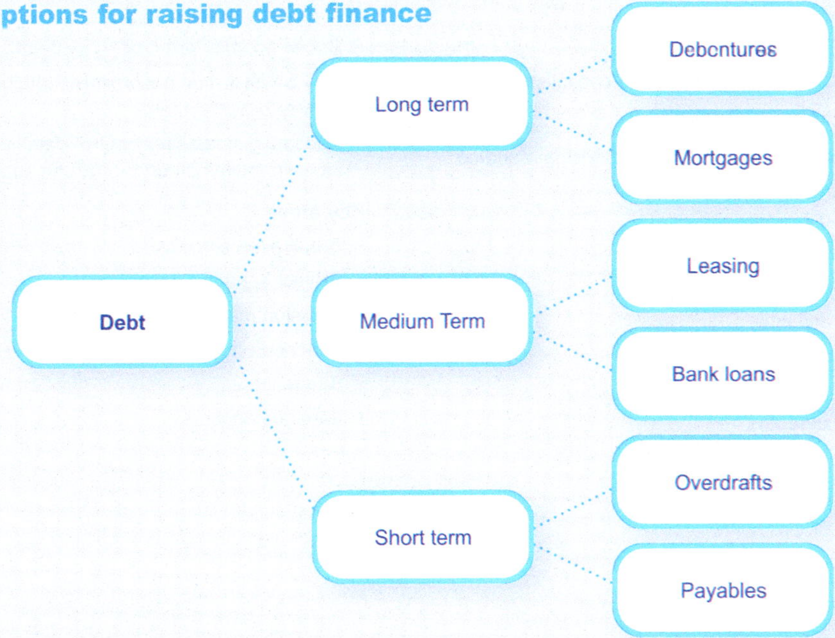

Other sources

- Government grants
- Business angels/venture capitalists
- Selling spare assets.

Factors to consider when choosing a source of finance

- Cost
- Availability
- Control
- Cash flow
- Security
- Gearing
- Exit routes

Cost accounting

- Based on standard costing systems
- May be based on absorption, marginal or activity based systems
- Becoming increasingly out-of-date in modern manufacturing environments

Key areas:

- Break even analysis
- Project appraisal
- Decision making
- Risk and uncertainty
- Budgeting
- Variance analysis

Break even analysis

$$\text{Break even point} = \frac{\text{Total Fixed Costs}}{\text{Contribution/unit}}$$

$$\text{Break even revenue} = \frac{\text{Total Fixed Costs}}{\text{Contribution margin}}$$

Margin of safety = Budgeted Sales – Break even sales

Key limitations

- Assumes a constant selling price
- Ignores (dis)economies of scale
- Difficult to cope with stepped fixed costs
- Only relevant in the short term.

Marginal decision making

- Accepting/rejecting special orders
- Closing a business unit
- Abandoning a project

Relevant costs and revenues must satisfy three criteria:

- Future
- Incremental
- Cash

Key problems:

- May need to consider opportunity costs
- The accounting (and tax) impact will be different

Investment appraisal

Method:	**Net Present Value (NPV)**
How to calculate:	Use a cost of capital and discount factors to discount future cash flows to give the present value
Best used when:	The project is long and the cost of capital is known
Key advantage:	Gives an absolute estimate of the impact on shareholder wealth
Key disadvantage:	Relies on a reliable cost of capital estimate
Method:	**Payback period**
How to calculate:	Determine how quickly the original cash injection is recovered
Best used when:	The project is short and/or cash is in short supply
Key advantage:	Provides a minimum target for project life
Key disadvantage:	Requires a target/benchmark

Method:	**Accounting Rate of Return (ARR)**
How to calculate:	Divide average profits by the initial investment
Best used when:	The project has profit targets to meet
Key advantage:	A simple calculation based on readily available Information
Key disadvantage:	Profits are easily manipulated
Method:	**Internal Rate of Return (IRR)**
How to calculate:	Determine the cost of capital that provides a zero NPV
Best used when:	The project is long and the cost of capital has not yet be determined
Key advantage:	Tells us the highest acceptable cost of capital
Key disadvantage:	It is not useful for comparing projects

Dealing with risk in decision making

An expected value summarises all the different possible outcomes by calculating a single weighted average. It is the long run average (though not necessarily the most likely result).

Complicated scenarios could be represented as a decision tree. Decision trees force the decision maker to consider the logical sequence of events.

Key limitations:

- Only useful for one-off decisions
- Based on subjective information
- Ignores attitudes to risk
- Does not provide an actual outcome

Budgeting

Effective budgetary control requires:

- a serious attitude is taken to the system
- clear demarcation between areas of managerial responsibility
- budget targets that are challenging yet achievable
- established data collection, analysis and reporting techniques
- reports aimed at individual managers
- fairly short reporting periods
- timely variance reports
- action being taken to get operations back under control if they are shown to be out of control.

Variance analysis

Key components of effective variance analysis:

- allocating responsibility
- keeping up-to-date standards
- flexing budgets for variable costs
- strong procedures for determining whether to investigate
- linking causes to the variance
- including feedforward control to improve future performance
- identifying trends which can be incorporated into strategic plans.

Other quantitative analysis techniques

- Linear regression
- Correlation
- Time series analysis

chapter

21

Managing strategic change

In this chapter

- Types of change.
- Preparing for change – Lewin.
- The change kaleidoscope.

Types of change

Speed of change	Extent of change: Transformation	Extent of change: Realignment
Incremental	**Evolution:** Transformational change implemented gradually through inter-related initiatives; likely to be proactive change undertaken in participation of the need for future change	**Adaptation:** Change undertaken to realign the way in which the organisation operates; implemented in a series of steps
Big bang	**Revolution:** Transformational change that occurs via simultaneous initiatives on many fronts: • more likely to be forced and reactive because of the changing competitive conditions that the organisation is facing	**Reconstruction:** Change undertaken to realign the way in which the organisation operates with many initiatives implemented simultaneously: • often forced and reactive because of a changing competitive context

Preparing for change – Lewin

Lewin suggests that change is achieved in three stages:

- Unfreeze

  Create the initial motivation to change by convincing staff of the undesirability of the present situation.

- Change

  Make the necessary changes to strategy, processes, culture etc.

- Refreeze

  Reinforcement of the new pattern of work or behaviour through rewards, praise, etc.

The change kaleidoscope (Balogun and Hope Hailey)

Contextual features:

- time
- scope
- preservation
- diversity
- capability
- capacity
- readiness
- power

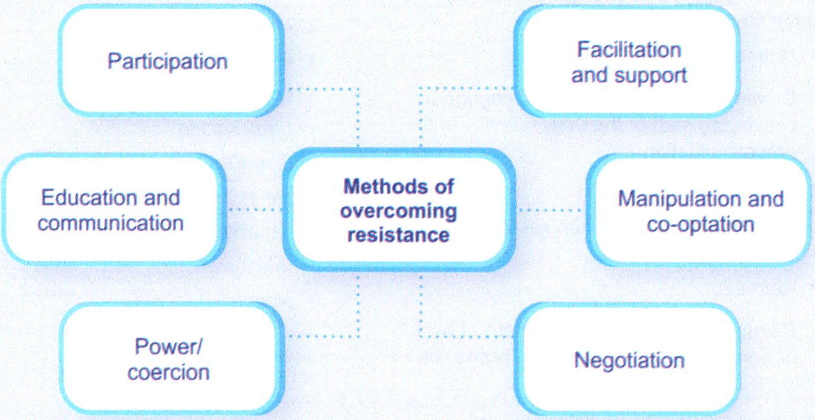
Participation
Facilitation and support
Education and communication
Methods of overcoming resistance
Manipulation and co-optation
Power/ coercion
Negotiation

Index

C

D

E

F

G

H

I

Q

R